THE KENNEDY ASSASSINATION

INTERPRETING PRIMARY DOCUMENTS

Charles W. Carey Jr., Book Editor

Bruce Glassman, Vice President
Bonnie Szumski, Publisher
Helen Cothran, Managing Editor

GREENHAVEN
PRESS ®

THOMSON
—★—™
GALE

San Diego • Detroit • New York • San Francisco • Cleveland
New Haven, Conn. • Waterville, Maine • London • Munich

LIBRARY OF CONGRESS CATALOGING-IN-PUBLICATION DATA

The Kennedy assassination / Charles W. Carey Jr., book editor.
    p. cm. — (Interpreting primary documents)
Includes bibliographical references and index.
ISBN 0-7377-2112-X (lib. bdg. : alk. paper)
    1. Kennedy, John F. (John Fitzgerald), 1917–1963—Assassination—Sources.
I. Carey, Charles W., Jr. II. Series.
E842.9.K46 2004
364.152'4'097309046—dc22

2004040610

CONTENTS

that Ruby's ability to penetrate Dallas police security meant that either he or the department itself might have been involved in Kennedy's assassination.

Chapter 2: The Nation and the World Respond

for their fallen president. On the first anniversary of Kennedy's death, many Americans felt worse than ever about the assassination.

Chapter 3: *The Warren Commission Report* and Its Supporters

Chapter 4: Negative Responses to *The Warren Commission Report*

FOREWORD

In a debate on the nature of the historian's task, the Canadian intellectual Michael Ignatieff wrote, "I don't think history is a lesson in patriotism. It should be a lesson in truth. And the truth is both painful and many-sided." Part of Ignatieff's point was that those who seek to understand the past should guard against letting prejudice or patriotism interfere with the truth. This point, although simple, is subtle. Everyone would agree that patriotism is no excuse for outright fabrication, and that prejudice should never induce a historian to deliberately lie or deceive. Ignatieff's concern, however, was not so much with deliberate falsification as it was with the way prejudice and patriotism can lead to selective perception, which can skew the judgment of even those who are sincere in their efforts to understand the past. The truth, especially about the how and why of historical events, is seldom simple, and those who wish to genuinely understand the past must be sensitive to its complexities.

Each of the anthologies in the Greenhaven Press Interpreting Primary Documents series strives to portray the events and attitudes of the past in all their complexity. Rather than providing a simple narrative of the events, each volume presents a variety of views on the issues and events under discussion and encourages the student to confront and examine the complexity that attends the genuine study of history.

Furthermore, instead of aiming simply to transmit information from historian to student, the series is designed to develop and train students to become historians themselves, by focusing on the interpretation of primary documents. Such documents, including newspaper articles, speeches, personal reflections, letters, diaries, memoranda, and official reports, are the raw material from which the historian refines an authentic understanding of the past. The anthology examining desegregation, for instance, includes the voices of presidents, state governors, and ordinary citizens, and draws from the *Congressional Record,* newspapers and magazines, letters, and books published at the time. The selections differ in scope and opinion as well, allowing the student to examine the issue of desegregation from a variety of perspectives. By looking frankly at the arguments offered by those in favor of racial segregation and by those opposed, for example, students can better understand those arguments, the people who advanced them, and the time in which they lived.

The structure of each book in the Interpreting Primary Documents series helps readers sharpen the critical faculties the serious study of history requires. A concise introduction outlines the era or event at hand and provides the necessary historical background. The chapters themselves begin with a preface containing a straightforward account of the events discussed and an overview of how these events can be interpreted in different ways by examining the different documents in the chapter. The selections, in turn, are chosen for their accessibility and relevance, and each is preceded by a short introduction offering historical context and a summary of the author's point of view. A set of questions to guide interpretation accompanies each article and encourages readers to examine the authors' prejudices, probe their assumptions, and compare and contrast the various perspectives offered in the chapter. Finally, a detailed timeline traces the development of key events, a comprehensive bibliography of selected secondary material guides further research, and a thorough index lets the reader quickly access relevant information.

As Ignatieff remarked, in the same debate in which he urged the historian to favor truth over blind patriotism, "History for me is the study of arguments." The Interpreting Primary Documents series is for readers eager to understand the arguments, and attitudes, that animated historical change.

INTRODUCTION

The assassination of President John Kennedy has been called the greatest murder mystery in U.S. history. Forty years later, the most likely explanation for Kennedy's death is the official one: Kennedy was shot by Lee Harvey Oswald, a lone gunman who in turn was shot by Jack Ruby, another lone gunman. But because of the irregularities surrounding the investigation of Kennedy's death, as well as a number of coincidences and oddities connected with the case that have never been satisfactorily explained, most Americans believe to this day that the Kennedy assassination was the result of some sort of conspiracy.

Climate of the Times

Kennedy's death took place during turbulent times. In 1963 the United States was in the middle of the Cold War with the Union of Soviet Socialist Republics (USSR). Ever since the Russian Revolution in 1917, Americans had feared that the Soviets intended to spread communism around the globe. For evidence, they pointed to the USSR's takeover of Eastern Europe and the rise of communism in China after World War II. Meanwhile, the Soviets were equally fearful of U.S. imperialism. For evidence, they pointed to the creation of the North Atlantic Treaty Organization, a U.S.-sponsored military alliance of Western European nations, the placing of nuclear warheads in Turkey on the USSR's southern border, and the reconstruction of Japan on the USSR's eastern flank. The two sides never had a war with one another, but they fought their war through proxies around the globe.

Despite having been Allies against Germany in World War II, the United States and the Soviet Union became adversaries almost as soon as the war ended. The Berlin crisis heightened tensions between the two superpowers. The former German capital was divided after World War II into Soviet and Western zones of occupation, but in 1948 the Soviets blockaded West Berlin in an effort to reunite it with Soviet-backed East Germany. The United States countered the blockade with an extensive and expensive airlift of food and fuel for West Berliners; it also beefed up its military forces in West Germany.

Relations were further strained by the outbreak of the Korean War in 1950, when the Soviet-backed North invaded the U.S.-backed South. Soviet troops never served during the Korean War, but U.S. troops did, as did troops from Communist China. Although the war ended in 1953, fifty years later American troops remain in South Korea to preserve the shaky cease-fire.

One of the last places the United States expected to fight the Cold War was in its own hemisphere. Ever since the days of President James Monroe, Americans had looked upon Latin America as a place where U.S. interests would always be well served. But in the late 1950s, the Communists found a base for the exportation of their creed in Cuba, just ninety miles off the coast of Florida.

The Cuban Revolution

In 1959, the year before Kennedy was elected president, rebel forces under Fidel Castro took control of Cuba. At first, Castro was not a Communist, and he asked the United States to support his regime. The United States refused, so Castro turned to the Soviets for help. Realizing that Soviet influence in Cuba might help offset U.S. influence in Western Europe, Turkey, and Japan, the Soviets eagerly offered Castro aid. As a result, Castro took Cuba down the road to communism, much to the shock of Americans, who lost millions of dollars in investments after the takeover.

Thousands of Cubans, most of them members of the upper and middle classes, fled Cuba after the 1959 revolution. Many of them settled in the United States, where they petitioned the U.S. government to help them reclaim their homeland. During the Kennedy administration, the Central

Intelligence Agency (CIA) harbored, supplied, and trained anti-Castro terrorists who attacked targets in Cuba. The CIA also attempted to back an anti-Castro coup and to assassinate Castro, all without success. The attempts outraged the Cuban leader, who eventually felt compelled to warn the United States that if the attacks did not stop he might retaliate by assassinating one or more U.S. leaders.

In 1961 the United States backed an invasion of Cuba by anti-Castro expatriate Cubans at the Bay of Pigs. The invasion was supposed to inspire the Cuban masses to rise up against their leader. Instead, the botched invasion served only to make Castro a hero in Cuba and around the world, thus making his position at home even more secure.

The Cuban Missile Crisis

Tensions worsened between Cuba—and by extension, the Soviet Union—and the United States in 1962, when the United States discovered that the Soviets were preparing to place nuclear missiles in Cuba. The United States demanded that the missile sites be dismantled, and the U.S. Navy blockaded Cuba until this was done. Part of the deal over the missiles' removal involved the United States' agreeing secretly to remove its warheads from Turkey as well as to give its solemn (but secret) assurances that it would not invade Cuba again.

As a result of Cold War machinations, most Americans were deeply concerned that Communists were plotting to overthrow the U.S. government. Because of events in Cuba surrounding the Cuban Revolution and the Cuban missile crisis, many Americans feared that Communist aggression, if and when it was directed against the United States, would emanate from Cuba at the instigation of Fidel Castro. Because of the extensive U.S. involvement in anti-Castro activity, their fear was not unreasonable.

Camelot

The tragedy of Kennedy's assassination was heightened by the fact that he was one of the most popular U.S. presidents ever. The youngest man ever elected to the presidency, at the time of his death he was only forty-six. Handsome, witty, and married to a stunningly attractive woman, the former Jacqueline Bouvier, Kennedy was also a decorated war hero and the author of a Pulitzer Prize–winning book.

Once in the White House, Kennedy's star continued to rise with the American people. He shocked the nation by publicly accepting the blame for the failed Bay of Pigs invasion since it happened while he was president, even though he had little to do with its planning or execution. Rather than turn against him for the invasion's failure, however, the nation embraced him for telling the truth. His popularity soared following the peaceful settlement of the Cuban missile crisis, and his tough stance against the spread of communism inspired confidence in millions of Americans.

Kennedy's public persona endeared him to the nation as well. Whereas previous presidents had cultivated images of themselves as sedate and genteel, Kennedy and his family played touch football on the White House lawn. One of the most popular recordings of the day poked good-natured fun at the president, and when Kennedy himself admitted to being amused by the recording, its popularity (and his) soared even higher. And yet, at the same time, the Kennedys were glamorous people who came as close as any family in the United States ever has to being royalty. The result of all this was what some observers have called Camelot, a reference to the mythical life and times of King Arthur, his lovely bride Guinevere, and the heroic Knights of the Round Table. In Camelot, Arthur and Guinevere presided over a wealthy and beautiful fairy-tale land while Arthur led his knights in combat against the dark forces of evil surrounding Camelot on all sides. In the 1960s version, the United States was Camelot, Kennedy was King Arthur, Jacqueline Kennedy was Guinevere, and Kennedy's brothers and advisers were the Knights of the Round Table.

The Assassination

Then, in the midst of this fairy tale, tragedy struck. On November 22, 1963, at approximately 12:30 P.M., President

Kennedy was shot and killed while riding in a motorcade through Dealey Plaza in downtown Dallas, Texas. Bullets pierced his back and neck and blew out a huge chunk of his head. Jacqueline Kennedy, who was riding beside him in the presidential limousine, was splattered with her husband's blood. At one point she tried to scramble onto the back of the car, some say in fear for her life, others say in an effort to retrieve a piece of Kennedy's skull. Texas governor John Connally, who was riding in the limousine in the seat in front of Kennedy, was wounded in the back, chest, wrist, and thigh, although he survived his injuries.

An eyewitness saw a man with a rifle on the sixth floor of the Texas School Book Depository Building, which the presidential motorcade had just passed. A search of the sixth

President Kennedy was popular with the press and the public. His assassination in November 1963 shocked the nation.

floor turned up a rifle and three spent cartridge shells but no shooter. The description of the rifleman was given to police, and a manhunt was organized.

At about 1:15 P.M., a Dallas police officer, J.D. Tippit, was shot and killed by an assailant whose description matched that of the rifleman in the sixth-floor window. At 1:50 P.M., Dallas police arrested a man fitting that description who was carrying the revolver that had been used to kill Tippit. The man was Lee Harvey Oswald.

Oswald the Prime Suspect

Oswald was born and raised in New Orleans, Louisiana. At the time of Kennedy's death, he was renting a room in Dallas while his wife lived in nearby Fort Worth. Oswald was an employee of the Texas School Book Depository, and he had been at work at the time of the shooting. During his interrogation by police, he denied owning the revolver that had been used to shoot Tippit, and he denied that he had shot either Tippit or the president. When his answers to a number of other questions proved to be similarly unconvincing, he was charged with Tippit's murder, and later with Kennedy's.

Oswald was held without bail in the Dallas police lockup for two days. On November 24, as he was being transferred by local law enforcement officials to the Dallas County jail, he was shot and killed by Jack Ruby, a Dallas nightclub owner, in the basement of the Dallas police headquarters. Ruby was arrested immediately; he eventually stood trial for murder and was sentenced to death, but he died in prison from cancer before the sentence could be carried out.

The World Responds

The entire world was shocked by Kennedy's assassination. As commander in chief of the U.S. military, Kennedy was the acknowledged leader of the so-called free world, that part of the globe where capitalism rather than communism held sway. People in other nations had come to admire, respect, and trust Kennedy, and his death now threatened to take away the feeling of security he had given them. Even Kennedy's most dedicated foes, Soviet leader Nikita Khrushchev and Cuban leader Fidel Castro, seemed concerned that Kennedy's death might mark a deterioration in relations between their nations and the United States.

Americans Respond

Nowhere, of course, was Kennedy more deeply mourned than in his own country. Everyday life came to a virtual standstill all across the United States as businesses closed and schools dismissed students early. Even the New York Stock Exchange closed early, the first time in its history that it had done so in response to a political event. Forty years later, people who were alive at the time of Kennedy's death, even though they might have been children at the time, can remember exactly where they were and what they were doing when they heard about Kennedy's assassination. Its impact on the American psyche was at least as great as that of the bombing of Pearl Harbor in 1941 or the terrorist attacks on the Pentagon and the World Trade Center in 2001.

Following the president's death, hundreds of thousands of Americans flocked to the Capitol Building in Washington, D.C., where Kennedy's body lay in state. Millions of Americans stayed glued to their television sets for the four days during which Kennedy's funeral was planned and held. During this time, the major networks omitted all commercials and canceled all entertainment features to broadcast virtually nothing other than news related to Kennedy's death and the political biographies of the fallen president and his successor, former vice president Lyndon Johnson. Virtually every American watched Kennedy's funeral on television from start to finish, thus making it the first major media event in U.S. history.

The Police and FBI Investigate

To the Dallas police and the Federal Bureau of Investigation (FBI), it seemed perfectly clear that the assassin was

Lee Harvey Oswald. Oswald's palm print was found on the rifle that was retrieved from the sixth floor of the Texas School Book Depository Building. Fibers from the shirt he was wearing the day of the assassination were similar to fibers found on the retrieved rifle. A photograph of him taken by his wife showed Oswald, who had qualified as a sharpshooter while serving in the U.S. Marine Corps, holding a rifle that looked just like the one retrieved by police. The photograph also showed Oswald holding a revolver similar to the one used to kill Officer Tippit. His fellow coworkers testified that on the day of the assassination, Oswald had brought to work a long and bulky package that could have been a rifle. A bullet found at Parkland Hospital proved to have been fired from the retrieved rifle. Based on this evidence, Oswald seemed to be guilty beyond the shadow of a doubt.

As for Jack Ruby, Oswald's assassin, it was known to the Dallas police, who frequented his nightclub, that he was a great admirer of the Kennedys. Witnesses testified that Ruby had been morose ever since the assassination, and he had even temporarily closed down his nightclub out of respect for the slain president. His claim that he had shot Oswald to prevent Mrs. Kennedy from having to return to Dallas to testify against her husband's murderer seemed believable to those who knew him. Consequently, the FBI and local police were convinced that the assassinations of Kennedy and Oswald were the work of two lone gunmen, Oswald and Ruby.

The Warren Commission Is Formed

Despite the open-and-shut case against Oswald, the American public seemed skeptical that Oswald had acted alone. Oswald had once defected to the Soviet Union, where he married Marina Prusakova, a Soviet citizen, and he was known to have distributed leaflets on behalf of the Fair Play for Cuba Committee, a pro-Castro organization. These involvements with the Communist enemies of the United States seemed to indicate the strong possibility that Oswald had been helped by either the Soviets or the Cubans, if not both. Many Americans became convinced that a conspiracy was involved in Kennedy's death after Ruby shot Oswald; how else, they reasoned, could Ruby have shot Oswald while Oswald was in the custody of the police?

President Johnson moved quickly to combat the rising fears of millions of Americans that their president had been killed by some sort of international conspiracy. On November 29, exactly one week after Kennedy's assassination, he ordered the formation of a blue-ribbon panel to investigate Kennedy's death. Officially designated the President's Commission on the Assassination of President John F. Kennedy, the panel became known as the Warren Commission, after its chairman, Earl Warren, chief justice of the U.S. Supreme Court. The other six members of the commission were: Allen Dulles, former director of the CIA; Representative Gerald Ford of Michigan, an influential House Republican and future president of the United States; Representative

Vice President Lyndon B. Johnson is sworn in as president aboard Air Force One, *following the assassination of John F. Kennedy.*

Hale Boggs of Louisiana, an influential House Democrat; John McCloy, former assistant secretary of defense and former president of the World Bank; Senator Richard Russell of Georgia, an influential Senate Democrat; and Senator John Cooper of Kentucky, an influential Senate Republican. The commission's staff included sixty-four members, most of them lawyers or Internal Revenue Service agents. It did not include any investigative agents, and so the commission relied on the FBI and the CIA to collect evidence.

From February until September 1964, the commission interviewed almost five hundred witnesses. Their testimony was compiled in fifteen volumes, while various exhibits, mostly FBI documents, were compiled in another eleven volumes. In late 1964, the commission summarized its findings in one 888-page volume known as *The Warren Commission Report*. In its final report, the commission concurred in the FBI's finding that Oswald and Ruby had each acted alone, and that no conclusive evidence existed to connect either man with a conspiracy of any kind.

The Warren Commission Report Is Praised

The Warren Commission Report was intended to provide the definitive answer to the question of who killed Kennedy. A number of people agreed that it did. Top legal experts in this country and abroad studied the report and hailed it for its thoroughness as well as for its speed. No one accepted everything the report stated as the gospel truth, and a number of experts still had questions about some of the more curious aspects of the assassination. Despite these reservations, a surprisingly large number of legal experts praised the commission for the job it had done and accepted the report as offering the most plausible explanation for how President Kennedy was killed.

The Warren Commission Report Is Challenged

Meanwhile, the report was being challenged by a number of parties, legal experts and otherwise. The most vociferous, although certainly not the only, challenger was Mark Lane, an attorney hired by Oswald's mother to clear her son's name. These challengers, known collectively as conspiracists, insisted that Kennedy's death was the work of some sort of conspiracy, although their theories as to the exact nature of that conspiracy range across a broad spectrum.

The Magic Bullet

Conspiracists point to several flaws in the commission's findings to substantiate their claims. The biggest flaw, in their opinion, is the so-called magic bullet theory. According to the commission, the bullet that pierced Kennedy's neck also hit Connally in the back, shattered a rib before exiting through his chest, and then hit his wrist and thigh. This bullet, known as Commission Exhibit (CE) 399, was found on Connally's stretcher at Parkland Hospital. Since CE 399 appears to the naked eye to be a pristine bullet, meaning that it looks as if it had not hit anything, conspiracists argue that it could not possibly have done all that the commission claims it did. Instead, conspiracists generally believe that it took at least four bullets to do all the damage that Kennedy and Connally received.

A little-known fact about the assassination is that a bystander, James Tague, was struck by a fragment from one of the bullets fired during the assassination. To conspiracists, Tague's wounding is further evidence that more than three bullets were fired, although it is entirely possible that Tague was struck by a fragment from the third bullet, the one that the commission acknowledges missed Kennedy and Connally entirely.

The Zapruder Film

Another major flaw is the visual record presented by various amateur films and photographs. The most notable of these productions is the Zapruder film, so named because it was shot by amateur photographer Abraham Zapruder. Photographs made from the film (the film itself was not shown to the public until 1975, and by then it had been altered) seem to show that the president jerked backward as soon as he was hit in the head. This is the opposite reaction one would expect from someone who had been shot from the back, the direction from which Oswald fired. Instead, it makes it look as if Kennedy was shot from the front, most likely from the direction of the grassy knoll, a landscaped hill to the west of the Texas School Book Depository Building.

A third major flaw is the fact that a number of witnesses claim to have heard one or more shots fired from the grassy knoll area, while several also claim to have seen a puff of smoke emanate from this area immediately after the shooting. Obviously, Oswald could not have fired from the grassy knoll, and so, argue the conspiracists, there must have been more than one shooter.

A fourth major flaw was Oswald's apparent lack of motive for shooting the president other than his pro-Communist leanings. Oswald had once defected to the Soviet Union, he was married to a Russian national, and he was an open admirer of Fidel Castro. These connections to Communist regimes indicated to many Americans that Oswald might have been an agent of either the Soviet Union or Cuba.

Addressing the Flaws in *The Warren Commission Report*

Several arguments have been offered, by a variety of experts and assassination buffs, in response to the four major flaws. As for the magic bullet theory, a microscopic examination of CE 399 shows that a considerable amount of metal from the bullet's nose is indeed missing. Whether or not enough metal is missing to explain Kennedy's neck injury and all of Connally's injuries is still being debated.

Kennedy's reaction to being shot has been explained in a way that is consistent with his having been hit from behind. A close viewing of the Zapruder film indicates that, for a split second after being shot, Kennedy did indeed slump forward. It has been suggested that the lurch backward was a spastic reaction that is consistent with having a major portion of the brain rendered dysfunctional. In other words,

Kennedy jerked backward for much the same reason that a chicken with its head cut off will occasionally run around the barnyard before collapsing.

Several arguments have been advanced to refute the theory that one or more shooters fired from the grassy knoll area. First, the grassy knoll is a wide-open area, and anyone firing from there would almost certainly have been seen by spectators in Dealey Plaza. Second, a number of observers, including at least one police officer, were stationed so that they overlooked the grassy knoll, and none of them reported seeing anything suspicious in that area.

The question of Oswald's motivation for shooting Kennedy was answered somewhat in 1977, when Priscilla Johnson McMillan's biography of the Oswalds, *Marina and Lee*, was published. According to McMillan, Marina Oswald had told her husband that Kennedy reminded her of an old boyfriend back in Russia. If so, then Oswald may have shot Kennedy simply out of blind jealousy.

Further Government Investigations

Because *The Warren Commission Report* was perceived by a number of its readers to be flawed, the commission's conclusion that Oswald and Ruby were lone gunmen was not accepted by the majority of the population. Over the next thirty-five years, various government agencies would undertake their own investigations into Kennedy's death. The most important of these investigations were conducted by Jim Garrison, the Rockefeller Commission, the House Select Committee on Assassinations (HSCA), and the Church Committee. Although not technically an investigation, the Assassination Records Review Board (ARRB) was commissioned to make available to the public a plethora of records pertaining to Kennedy's death, so that anyone with the time and interest can decide for themselves who shot Kennedy.

The Garrison Investigation

Earling Carothers "Jim" Garrison was the district attorney for Orleans Parish, Louisiana, a jurisdiction which includes the city of New Orleans. In 1967 Garrison began investigating the possibility that anti-Castro CIA operatives based in a training camp in Lacombe, a small town in Orleans Parish, might have been involved in a plot to assassinate Kennedy. Garrison's chief suspect was David Ferrie, a trainer at the camp and a private investigator for New Orleans mobster Carlos Marcello. After Ferrie committed suicide just days before being arrested, Garrison put together a case against Clay Shaw, a wealthy New Orleans businessman and former CIA operative who had reported for the agency on activities throughout Latin America. Later, it was discovered that Shaw sat on the board of directors of Permindex, a company that had been implicated in an assassination attempt on French leader Charles de Gaulle. Garrison alleged that Shaw, Ferrie, and Oswald, among others, had plotted to set up a triangulation of gunfire—meaning multiple shooters—as a means of killing Kennedy.

The Orleans Parish grand jury indicted Shaw after considering Garrison's case against him, and Shaw was arrested in 1967. Two years later his case came to trial. By then, a number of witnesses had died or changed their testimony. Garrison claims that the CIA attempted to cover up its involvement with Shaw, and by implication Kennedy's death, by infiltrating Garrison's operation, stealing his files, and tampering with his witnesses. In March 1969, the jury in Shaw's trial decided that Shaw was innocent, but it did agree with Garrison that a conspiracy to kill Kennedy had been underfoot. Garrison's investigation eventually formed the basis for Oliver Stone's controversial 1991 movie, *JFK*.

The Rockefeller Commission

The President's Commission on CIA Activities Within the United States was formed in 1975 by order of President Gerald Ford, a former Warren Commission member. Chaired by Vice President Nelson Rockefeller and known as the Rockefeller Commission, its task was to investigate allegations of wrongdoing by the CIA, particularly in conjunction with the Watergate scandal. During the course of the investigation, the commission considered allegations that the CIA had played a role in Kennedy's assassination. Specifically, it had been alleged that E. Howard Hunt and Frank Sturgis, two of the Watergate burglars, had shot Kennedy from the grassy knoll while employed by the CIA. The commission's final report refutes the notion that Hunt and Sturgis, or anyone else, shot at Kennedy from the grassy knoll. However, the commission's entire proceedings were generally considered to be a whitewash, at least of the CIA's domestic activities.

The Church Committee

While the Rockefeller Commission was focusing on the CIA, the U.S. Senate began to investigate the entire U.S. intelligence community. A select Senate committee, known as the Church Committee after the name of its chairman, Senator Frank Church, took a deep look into the activities of the FBI, the CIA, the National Security Agency, the Internal Revenue Service, and similar agencies. Among other things, the committee hoped to shed light on how these agencies had handled the investigation of Kennedy's assassination.

By the time the committee finished its work in 1976, it had concluded that Kennedy most likely did not die at the hands of a conspiracy. However, the committee noted that the intelligence agencies did a poor job of investigating the possibility that Kennedy had been killed by one or more agents of a foreign government. This possibility seems rather likely in light of the CIA's attempts to assassinate several foreign leaders, including Cuba's Fidel Castro, who had threatened to retaliate in kind if the attempts did not stop. The committee expressed some concern that the Warren Commission had not even been told about the CIA's involvement in foreign assassinations, because if it had the Warren Commission almost certainly would have investigated this aspect more closely.

The 1975 showing of the Zapruder film on national television created a huge public stir because it seemed to confirm that Kennedy had been shot from the front, not from the back as the Warren Commission had claimed. As a result, the U.S. House of Representatives decided to conduct its own investigation into Kennedy's death, while also investigating the assassinations of Robert Kennedy and Martin Luther King Jr. In 1976 the House established a select committee and empowered it to look into every detail of the circumstances surrounding these three assassinations. In terms of the Kennedy assassination, the committee was asked to pass judgment on the work of the Warren Commission.

Unlike the Warren Commission, the HSCA took seriously the testimony of dozens of witnesses who claimed that at least one shot was fired from the grassy knoll. Eventually, the committee came up with an audiotape that reportedly had recorded the events in Dealey Plaza over a police radio channel. The audiotape was submitted to acoustical experts who concluded that the tape records at least one gunshot fired from the direction of the grassy knoll. Based on this evidence, the HSCA concluded that Kennedy had died at the hands of a conspiracy.

Unfortunately, the HSCA's efforts did little to clear up the mystery surrounding Kennedy's death. It vaguely attributed the conspiracy to organized crime, which supposedly wanted Kennedy dead because he had ordered the FBI and the Justice Department to crack down on mob-related criminal activity. However, the HSCA also concluded that neither of the two mobsters most likely to have organized a conspiracy, Carlos Marcello and Santos Trafficante, had anything to do with Kennedy's death. More damning to the HSCA's work was the revelation several years later that the audiotape upon which it had relied so heavily actually contained recordings of events that were far removed from Dealey Plaza, and that it contained no gunshots.

The Assassination Records Review Board
The movie *JFK* created such a stir that Congress felt compelled to take a step that the conspiracists had been demanding for years—declassify and make available to the

public all documents pertaining to Kennedy's death. In 1992 Congress passed the President John F. Kennedy Assassination Records Collection Act, better known as the JFK Act. This act established the ARRB and tasked it to locate and publish as many documents related to the assassination as it could. The five-member board went to work in 1994, and over the next four years its staff ferreted out a number of government documents and interviewed many witnesses to determine the authenticity of those documents. The ARRB's final report was released to the public in 1998; it had been preceded by reams of declassified documents pertaining to Kennedy's death.

The ARRB's mission was not to reinvestigate the assassination, but in the process of doing its job it discovered a number of anomalies associated with Kennedy's autopsy. According to the ARRB, it appears that photographs and X-rays were altered, notes were destroyed, and crucial elements of a typical autopsy were not even conducted. The ARRB never concluded from these anomalies that the federal government had attempted to cover up the details of Kennedy's wounds. However, its final report makes it difficult to escape drawing that conclusion.

Who Shot Kennedy?

Forty years after the Kennedy assassination, the most reasonable answer to this question is "Lee Harvey Oswald, acting alone." Nevertheless, a majority of Americans believe that Kennedy's death was somehow the work of a conspiracy. Many groups and individuals have been suspected of putting together such a conspiracy, but the four leading suspects are organized crime, the CIA, the military-industrial complex, and an international web of fascists. Oddly enough, the Soviets and the Cubans, who at the time seemed the most likely suspects to have conspired against Kennedy, have been virtually ignored by conspiracists, mostly because no evidence has surfaced linking them to Kennedy's murder.

Under the leadership of President Kennedy and his brother

Robert, who was the attorney general, the federal government had begun to crack down on organized crime. One victim of the crackdown was Carlos Marcello, head of the Mafia family that controlled New Orleans and Dallas. Marcello claimed that in 1961 he was kidnapped by government agents and deported to Guatemala. Upon returning to the United States (he was flown back by David Ferrie, the prime suspect in Jim Garrison's investigation), Marcello supposedly began plotting Kennedy's death with several other gangsters.

Marcello had connections to Oswald and Jack Ruby. Oswald's uncle, Charles "Dutz" Murret, had once worked for Marcello; Oswald's mother had dated several of Marcello's men; and Oswald himself had reportedly worked for Marcello as a numbers runner. Ruby was a personal acquaintance of Joseph Civillo, who headed up Marcello's operations in Dallas.

A number of stories have circulated to the effect that Marcello and another mob leader, Santos Trafficante, had arranged for Kennedy's death. Several of these stories have been told by men claiming to have pulled the trigger that killed Kennedy. However, the HSCA, which concluded that organized crime was involved in some way in Kennedy's murder, was unable to uncover enough evidence to pin the blame for Kennedy's death on Marcello or any other mobster.

The CIA

Kennedy did not get along with the CIA any better than he did with the mob. Supposedly, a number of CIA operatives were incensed when Kennedy canceled U.S. air support for the Bay of Pigs invasion, which was carried out by CIA agents and expatriate Cubans. At the same time, Kennedy was hardly pleased with the CIA's planning and execution of the invasion. According to several sources, he was considering dissolving the CIA because it seemed to be beyond the federal government's control. The CIA had plotted the assassinations of several foreign leaders, and at the time of Kennedy's death it was plotting to assassinate Cuba's Fidel Castro. Several of the subjects in Jim Garrison's investigation, specifically David Ferrie and Clay Shaw, were former CIA operatives.

The Military-Industrial Complex

In the late 1950s, President Dwight Eisenhower warned Americans that the U.S. military and defense contractors had become a dangerously powerful special interest. According to some conspiracists, the military-industrial complex was responsible for Kennedy's death because he opposed their plans to escalate the war in Vietnam. This theory cites as evidence the fact that Kennedy's successor, Lyndon Johnson, significantly increased U.S. involvement in Vietnam upon taking over the Oval Office. Some conspiracists believe that Johnson himself ordered the hit on Kennedy and that Johnson provided the conspirators with inside information as to how Kennedy would be protected by the Secret Service during his visit to Texas. Supposedly, Johnson had learned that he was going to be dropped from the Democratic ticket in 1964, and he saw killing Kennedy as his last chance to achieve his ambition of becoming president.

An International Web of Fascists

One of Kennedy's most vocal critics was H.L. Hunt, a Texas oil billionaire. Hunt spent millions of dollars of his own money to spread anti-Communist propaganda and to maintain his own intelligence network, which had contacts with various government intelligence agencies. Hunt was outraged at Kennedy because Kennedy was threatening to abolish a tax loophole known as the oil-depletion allowance, a move that would cost Hunt and his fellow oilmen millions. On the day that Kennedy was shot, a full-page advertisement that was highly critical of Kennedy's policies appeared in a Dallas newspaper. The ad was paid for by Hunt and his colleagues.

Hunt may have had ties, albeit tenuous, with Permindex, an international finance corporation headquartered in Switzerland that had helped finance two assassination attempts on French leader Charles de Gaulle in 1961 and

1962. One of Permindex's directors was Clay Shaw, one of the subjects of Jim Garrison's investigation. According to one source, Permindex was linked with the American Council of Christian Churches (ACCC), a front for various spying and propaganda activities of the FBI. At the time of Kennedy's death, Hunt was the ACCC's acting director.

Decide for Yourself

The Warren Commission's conclusion that Oswald and Ruby each acted alone remains the best explanation for the events surrounding Kennedy's death. However, enough circumstantial evidence exists to call into question that explanation. Ultimately, anyone interested in getting to the bottom of the Kennedy assassination must examine the documents that the ARRB has made public and make their own informed decision.

1

THE ASSASSINATION

CHAPTER PREFACE

On November 22, 1963, President John Kennedy was shot and killed while riding in a presidential motorcade through downtown Dallas, Texas. Also wounded in the attack were Texas governor John Connally, who was riding in the limousine with Kennedy, and James Tague, a Dallas resident who was watching the motorcade.

Kennedy was murdered in front of hundreds of witnesses, including his wife Jacqueline, who rode in the limousine beside him. Several witnesses reported seeing a rifle extending from a sixth-floor window of the Texas School Book Depository Building, which Kennedy's limousine had just passed. One witness actually got a good enough look at the shooter to be able to describe him to police. Within hours, a suspect matching the description of the shooter was arrested in a Dallas theater on suspicion of killing J.D. Tippit, a Dallas police officer who had tried to apprehend him.

The suspect was Lee Harvey Oswald. Oswald was an employee of the Texas School Book Depository, and he had qualified as a sharpshooter while serving in the U.S. Marine Corps. After several hours of questioning, he was arrested and charged with the deaths of Kennedy and Tippit.

For two days, it seemed as if the police had an open-and-shut case against Oswald. But then, on November 24, as Oswald was being transferred from one lockup to another, he was shot and killed in the basement of the Dallas police headquarters by Jack Ruby, a local nightclub owner. Ruby's ability to penetrate police security suddenly raised the possibility that Kennedy had been killed by a conspiracy.

Indeed, the facts around the shooting of the president were never as cut-and-dried as the police might have hoped. Dealey Plaza, where the shooting took place, is surrounded by a variety of structures that causes sounds to reverberate in strange ways, and eyewitnesses could not even agree on how many shots were fired. Nor could they agree on the direction from which the shots had been fired, further confusing the situation and giving more credence to the possibility of a conspiracy.

The President Is Shot

Associated Press

When President Kennedy was shot, total chaos broke out. The president's car was whisked to Parkland Hospital, where a team of local physicians was unable to save his life and, indeed, seemed unsure as to the exact nature of the president's wounds. Secret Service agents and federal and local law enforcement officials searched frantically for the assassin, in the process rounding up whatever suspects could be found. Nevertheless, early reports seemed consistent about two things: Several citizens reported hearing three shots, while several others reported seeing a rifle being retracted into a sixth-floor window of the Texas School Book Depository Building. In time, these reports would form the basis for the government's official version of the assassination.

Most Americans read about the assassination the next day in their local newspapers, which pieced the story together from wire reports from the Associated Press. This article, an excerpt from the *Lynchburg News*, presents the facts of the assassination as they were known at the time.

As you read, consider the following questions:
1. To what degree does this article make the case that the president was shot by a lone gunman?
2. To what degree does this article suggest that the shooter had one or more accomplices?

A furtive sniper armed with a high-powered rifle assassinated President John F. Kennedy here Friday. Barely two hours after Kennedy's death, Lyndon B. Johnson took the oath of office as the 36th president of the United States.

Associated Press, "Sniper's Bullet Kills President," *Lynchburg (Virginia) News*, November 23, 1963. Copyright © 1963 by The Associated Press. Reproduced by permission.

Kennedy was shot through the head and neck as he rode through Dallas in the presidential limousine in what had been a triumphal motorcade.

When the shots were fired at about 12:30 P.M. and the chief executive slumped forward, Mrs. Kennedy turned in the seat and cried, "Oh, no," in anguish and horror.

She tried to cradle his head in her arms as the limousine took off at top speed for Parkland Hospital where Kennedy died about half an hour later.

Johnson, who was Kennedy's vice president, automatically succeeded to the presidency.

The new chief executive took the oath of office at about 2:39 P.M. Central Standard Time. For the first time in history, the oath was administered by a woman—U.S. Dist. Judge Sarah T. Hughes.

Johnson was sworn in aboard the presidential jet transport—Air Force One—at Dallas' Love Field. He then flew to Washington to take over the government which Kennedy had directed since Jan. 20, 1961. Kennedy's body was aboard the plane.

The same volley of shots that killed the President struck Gov. John B. Connally of Texas, who was riding with Kennedy.

Like Kennedy, the stricken Connally was sped to Parkland Hospital and wheeled into surgery for an emergency operation. The Democratic governor was struck in the body and wrist.

Kennedy, who was 46, was cut down by a flurry of bullets shortly after his open-topped car had left the Dallas business district, where thousands had massed 10 to 12 deep along each curb to cheer him and Mrs. Kennedy.

This was the first presidential assassination since 1901 when a half-crazed gunman shot William McKinley at close range during a reception in Buffalo, N.Y.

Kennedy was the first president to die in office since Franklin D. Roosevelt succumbed to a cerebral hemorrhage in April 1945.

The Secret Service, the Federal Bureau of Investigation

and Dallas police swung into action within seconds and launched what was perhaps the biggest, determined man-hunt in the nation's history.

A number of suspects were picked up during the next few hours.

Last Rites

Kennedy was administered the last rites of the Roman Catholic Church shortly after he was carried into Parkland Hospital. He was the nation's first Catholic president.

Emergency treatment given the dying President was described for newsmen by two physicians, Drs. Kemp Clark, 38, and Malcolm Perry, 34.

Dr. Perry said Kennedy suffered a neck wound—a bullet hole in the lower part of the neck. There was a second wound in Kennedy's head but Perry was not certain whether it was inflicted by the same bullet.

The physician said the President lost consciousness as soon as he was hit and never revived.

Kennedy speaks to a crowd on the morning of November 22, 1963. Later that day, he was shot and killed as his motorcade drove through downtown Dallas.

No Hope

"We never had any hope of saving his life," said Perry, though eight or ten physicians attended him in a frantic but futile effort to keep Kennedy alive.

Clark, a brain surgeon, reported that Kennedy was given oxygen and blood transfusions, then was administered an anaesthetic so an emergency tracheotomy could be performed.

During this procedure, surgeons cut a hole in the President's windpipe in an attempt to ease his breathing.

Perry said that shortly after he reached the hospital, the chief executive's heart action failed and "there was no palpable pulse beat."

The time of death was announced officially as 1 P.M. CST.

Police believed the fatal volley was fired from a textbook warehouse overlooking the expressway down which the President's car was heading.

Bob Jackson, a photographer for the Dallas Times Herald, heard one shot, then two rapid bursts as he rode in an open convertible in the presidential motorcade.

He said he looked up and saw two men peering from an upper-story window of the warehouse. As he looked, he said, he saw a rifle being drawn quickly back into a sixth-floor window. . . .

Eyewitness Account

The horror of the assassination was mirrored in an eyewitness account by Sen. Ralph Yarborough, who had been riding three cars behind Kennedy.

"You could tell something awful and tragic had happened," the senator told newsmen before Kennedy's death became known. His voice was breaking and his eyes were red-rimmed.

"I could see a Secret Service man in the President's car leaning on the car with his hands in anger, anguish and despair. I knew then something tragic had happened," Yarborough said.

Yarborough had counted three rifle shots as the presidential limousine left downtown Dallas through a triple underpass. The shots were fired from above—possibly from one of the bridges or from a nearby building.

Saw Gun Emerge

One witness, television reporter Mal Couch, said he saw a gun emerge from an upper story of a warehouse commanding an unobstructed view of the presidential car.

Kennedy was the first president to be assassinated since William McKinley was shot in 1901.

It was the first death of a president in office since Franklin D. Roosevelt succumbed to a cerebral hemorrhage at Warm Springs, Ga., in April 1945.

Dallas motorcycle officers, ranged around the cavalcade, took off across a field in the direction from which the murderer may have fired.

One officer raced to the foot of a nearby railroad embankment and climbed to the tracks above, gun in hand.

Pandemonium

The motorcade, which had just passed through downtown crowds standing 10 to 12 deep along each curb, broke apart in pandemonium as Secret Service agents rushed Kennedy and Connally to the hospital.

Ironically, Kennedy was shot to death at a spot where there were few spectators—after driving almost within handshaking distance of many thousands.

Kennedy's body was removed from Parkland Hospital at 2:05 P.M. in an ambulance with off-white curtains tightly drawn.

Mrs. Kennedy rode in a passenger seat in the ambulance.

Sense of Dread

An ominous sense of dread had struck the reporters, however, within seconds after the shooting. It was apparent that the neatly-ordered motorcade was falling apart and that city police were leaving the route in haste.

A crowd of stunned Dallas citizens thronged around the hospital where Kennedy died. The ambulance which took the body from the institution was forced almost to a halt at one point because of the silent, waiting people.

Adding poignancy to the tragedy was the fact that both Kennedy children will have birthdays within the next week. Caroline will be 6 on Nov. 27 and John F. Jr. will be 3 on Nov. 25.

On Goodwill Tour

The President had flown to Texas on a goodwill tour, speaking to citizens in the major cities and—never one to neglect practical politics—doing what he could to quiet partisan infighting among Texas Democrats.

The President and his aides had been very pleased with the way the trip had been going. In fact, a crowd of tens of thousands that saw Kennedy drive through Dallas toward his rendezvous with death was the largest and most enthusiastic of the journey.

In the 24 hours before he was murdered, Kennedy was seen and enthusiastically cheered by several hundred thousand Texans in San Antonio, Houston, Fort Worth and Dallas.

"Oh, My God, They Have Shot My Husband"

Jacqueline Kennedy, interviewed by Earl Warren and J. Lee Rankin

At the time President Kennedy was shot, no one was closer to him than his wife, Jacqueline Kennedy. Mrs. Kennedy was sitting in the backseat with her husband and to his immediate left at the moment he was hit. Accordingly, the Warren Commission felt that she might have a good idea as to where the shots that killed her husband came from. In addition, the commission believed that Mrs. Kennedy was the best source of information as to what transpired in the presidential limousine immediately before and after the shooting.

This article presents Mrs. Kennedy's testimony before the Warren Commission. Due to the sensitive nature of the questions, her testimony was given in her home in Georgetown in the District of Columbia, in the company of her brother-in-law, Attorney General Robert Kennedy. The only members of the commission who were present to hear her testify were Chief Justice Earl Warren, the commission's chairman; J. Lee Rankin, the commission's chief counsel; and an unidentified court reporter.

As you read, consider the following questions:
1. What does Mrs. Kennedy's testimony suggest about the possibility that shots were fired from a location other than the Texas School Book Depository Building, from which Lee Harvey Oswald allegedly fired three shots?
2. What do Mrs. Kennedy's remarks immediately following her husband's being shot suggest about the possibility that President Kennedy died as the result of a conspiracy?

Jacqueline Kennedy, testimony before the Warren Commission, Washington, DC, 1964.

The Chairman. The Commission will be in order. Mrs. Kennedy, the Commission would just like to have you say in your own words, in your own way, what happened at the time of the assassination of the President. Mr. Rankin will ask you a few questions, just from the time you left the airport until the time you started for the hospital. And we want it to be brief. We want it to be in your own words and want you to say anything that you feel is appropriate to that occasion.

Would you be sworn, please, Mrs. Kennedy?

Do you solemnly swear that the testimony you give before the Commission will be the truth, the whole truth, and nothing but the truth, so help you God?

Mrs. Kennedy. I do.

The Chairman. Would you be seated.

Mr. Rankin. State your name for the record.

Mrs. Kennedy. Jacqueline Kennedy.

Mr. Rankin. And you are the widow of the former President Kennedy?

Mrs. Kennedy. That is right.

Mr. Rankin. You live here in Washington?

Mrs. Kennedy. Yes.

The Trip to Dallas

Mr. Rankin. Can you go back to the time that you came to Love Field on Nov. 22 and describe what happened there after you landed in the plane?

Mrs. Kennedy. We got off the plane. The then Vice President and Mrs. Johnson were there. They gave us flowers. And then the car was waiting, but there was a big crowd there, all yelling, with banners and everything. And we went to shake hands with them. It was a very hot day. And you went all along a long line. I tried to stay close to my husband and lots of times you get pushed away, you know, people leaning over and pulling your hand. They were very friendly.

And, finally, I don't know how we got back to the car. I

think Congressman Thomas[1] somehow was helping me. There was lots of confusion.

Mr. Rankin. Then you did get into the car. And you sat on the left side of the car, did you, and your husband on your right?

Mrs. Kennedy. Yes.

Mr. Rankin. And was Mrs. Connally—

Mrs. Kennedy. In front of me.

Mr. Rankin. And Governor Connally to your right in the jump seat?

Mrs. Kennedy. Yes.

Mr. Rankin. And Mrs. Connally was in the jump seat?

Mrs. Kennedy. Yes.

Mr. Rankin. And then did you start off on the parade route?

Mrs. Kennedy. Yes.

Mr. Rankin. And were there many people along the route that you waved to?

Mrs. Kennedy. Yes. It was rather scattered going in.

Once there was a crowd of people with a sign saying something like "President Kennedy, please get out and shake our hands, our neighbors said you wouldn't."

Mr. Rankin. Did you?

Mrs. Kennedy. And he stopped and got out. That was, you know, like a little suburb and there were not many crowds. But then the crowds got bigger as you went in.

Large Crowds on the Streets

Mr. Rankin. As you got into the main street of Dallas were there very large crowds on all the streets?

Mrs. Kennedy. Yes.

Mr. Rankin. And you waved to them and proceeded down the street with the motorcade?

Mrs. Kennedy. Yes. And in the motorcade, you know, I usually would be waving mostly to the left side and he was waving mostly to the right, which is one reason you are not

1. Albert Thomas, a congressman from Texas

looking at each other very much. And it was terribly hot. Just blinding all of us.

Mr. Rankin. Now, do you remember as you turned off of the main street onto Houston Street?

Mrs. Kennedy. I don't know the name of the street.

Mr. Rankin. That is that one block before you get to the Depository Building.

Mrs. Kennedy. Well, I remember whenever it was, Mrs. Connally said, "We will soon be there." We could see a tunnel in front of us. Everything was really slow then. And I remember thinking it would be so cool under that tunnel.

Mr. Rankin. And then do you remember as you turned off of Houston onto Elm right by the Depository Building?

Mrs. Kennedy. Well, I don't know the names of the streets, but I suppose right by the Depository is what you are talking about?

The motorcade passes through downtown Dallas moments before the assassination. Jacqueline Kennedy later testified before the Warren Commission.

Mr. Rankin. Yes; that is the street that sort of curves as you go down under the underpass.

Mrs. Kennedy. Yes; well, that is when she said to President Kennedy, "You certainly can't say that the people of Dallas haven't given you a nice welcome."

Mr. Rankin. What did he say?

Mrs. Kennedy. I think he said—I don't know if I remember it or I have read it, "No, you certainly can't," or something. And you know then the car was very slow and there weren't very many people around.

And then—do you want me to tell you what happened?

Mr. Rankin. Yes; if you would, please.

Mrs. Kennedy. You know, there is always noise in a motorcade and there are always motorcycles beside us, a lot of them backfiring. So I was looking to the left. I guess there was a noise, but it didn't seem like any different noise really because there is so much noise, motorcycles and things. But then suddenly Governor Connally was yelling, "Oh, no, no, no."

Mr. Rankin. Did he turn toward you?

Mrs. Kennedy. No; I was looking this way, to the left, and I heard these terrible noises. You know. And my husband never made any sound. So I turned to the right. And all I remember is seeing my husband, he had this sort of quizzical look on his face, and his hand was up, it must have been his left hand. And just as I turned and looked at him, I could see a piece of his skull and I remember it was flesh colored. I remember thinking he just looked as if he had a slight headache. And I just remember seeing that. No blood or anything.

And then he sort of did this [indicating], put his hand to his forehead and fell in my lap.

And then I just remember falling on him and saying, "Oh, no, no, no," I mean, "Oh, my God, they have shot my husband." And "I love you, Jack," I remember I was shouting. And just being down in the car with his head in my lap. And it just seemed an eternity.

You know, then, there were pictures later on of me

climbing out the back. But I don't remember that at all.

Mr. Rankin. Do you remember Mr. Hill[2] coming to try to help on the car?

Mrs. Kennedy. I don't remember anything. I was just down like that.

And finally I remember a voice behind me, or something, and then I remember the people in the front seat, or somebody, finally knew something was wrong, and a voice yelling, which must have been Mr. Hill, "Get to the hospital," or maybe it was Mr. Kellerman,[3] in the front seat. But someone yelling. I was just down and holding him. [Reference to wounds deleted.]

Mrs. Kennedy Heard Two Shots

Mr. Rankin. Do you have any recollection of whether there were one or more shots?

Mrs. Kennedy. Well, there must have been two because the one that made me turn around was Governor Connally yelling. And it used to confuse me because first I remembered there were three and I used to think my husband didn't make any sound when he was shot. And Governor Connally screamed. And then I read the other day that it was the same shot that hit them both. But I used to think if I only had been looking to the right I would have seen the first shot hit him, then I could have pulled him down, and then the second shot would not have hit him. But I heard Governor Connally yelling and that made me turn around, and as I turned to the right my husband was doing this [indicating with hand at neck]. He was receiving a bullet. And those are the only two I remember.

And I read there was a third shot. But I don't know. Just those two.

Mr. Rankin. Do you have any recollection generally of the speed that you were going, not any precise amount?

Mrs. Kennedy. We were really slowing turning the corner. And there were very few people.

2. Secret Service agent Clinton J. Hill   3. Secret Service agent Roy Kellerman

Mr. Rankin. And did you stop at any time after the shots, or proceed about the same way?

Mrs. Kennedy. I don't know, because—I don't think we stopped. But there was such confusion. And I was down in the car and everyone was yelling to get to the hospital and you could hear them on the radio, and then suddenly I remember a sensation of enormous speed, which must have been when we took off.

Mr. Rankin. And then from there you proceeded as rapidly as possible to the hospital, is that right?

Mrs. Kennedy. Yes.

Mr. Rankin. Do you recall anyone saying anything else during the time of the shooting?

Mrs. Kennedy. No; there weren't any words. There was just Governor Connally's. And then I suppose Mrs. Connally was sort of crying and covering her husband. But I don't remember any words.

And there was a big windshield between—you know—I think. Isn't there?

Mr. Rankin. Between the seats.

Mrs. Kennedy. So you know, those poor men in the front, you couldn't hear them.

Mr. Rankin. Can you think of anything more?

The Chairman. No; I think not. I think that is the story and that is what we came for.

We thank you very much, Mrs. Kennedy.

Mr. Rankin. I would just like to ask if you recall Special Agent Kellerman saying anything to you as you came down the street after you turned that corner you referred to.

Mrs. Kennedy. You mean before the shots?

Mr. Rankin. Yes.

Mrs. Kennedy. Well, I don't, because—you know, it is very hard for them to talk. But I do not remember, just as I don't recall climbing out on the back of the car.

Mr. Rankin. Yes. You have told us what you remember about the entire period as far as you can recall, have you?

Mrs. Kennedy. Yes.

The Chairman. Thank you very much, Mrs. Kennedy.

Three Witnesses Tell What They Saw and Heard

Jack Bell, Norman Similas, and Alan Smith

President Kennedy was shot in plain view of almost three hundred witnesses. Most of them were ordinary citizens who had come out to watch a presidential motorcade. Many of these witnesses never testified as to what they saw or heard; instead, they simply wandered off in disbelief and shared their stories only with their families, friends, and coworkers. But a number of them did give their impressions as to what had happened in Dealey Plaza.

This excerpt comes from an article that appeared in the *New York Times* the day after the assassination. In it, three ordinary citizens—Jack Bell, a reporter for the Associated Press; Norman Similas, a Canadian businessman; and Alan Smith, a middle school student—give their impressions of the president's death. Although their stories jibe in some respects, in others they do not. Taken together, they offer an interesting perspective on how people who have witnessed the same thing can come away with different impressions of what they witnessed.

As you read, consider the following questions:
1. To what degree do these three eyewitness statements support the conclusion that Kennedy was shot by a lone gunman from the Texas School Book Depository Building?
2. To what degree do these statements support the conclusion that Kennedy was shot by multiple gunmen firing from multiple locations?

New York Times, "Eyewitnesses Describe Scene of Assassination," November 23, 1963. Copyright © 1963 by The New York Times Company. Reproduced by permission.

JACK BELL, AP REPORTER:
There was a loud bang as though a giant firecracker had exploded in the caverns between the tall buildings we were just leaving behind us.

In quick succession there were two other loud reports.

The ominous sound of these dismissed from the minds of us riding in the reporters' "pool" car the fleeting idea that some Texan was adding a bit of noise to the cheering welcome Dallas had given John F. Kennedy.

The reports sounded like rifle shots.

The man in front of me screamed, "My God, they're shooting at the President!"

Our driver braked the car sharply and we swung the doors open to leap out. Suddenly the procession, which had halted, shot forward again.

In the flash of that instant, a little tableau was enacted in front of a colonnade toward which the velvety green grass swelled upward to a small park[1] near the top of an underpass for which we had been headed.

Cars Speed Ahead

A man was pushing a woman dressed in bright orange to the ground and seemed to be falling protectively over her. A photographer, scrambling on all fours toward the crest of the rise, held a camera trained in their direction.

As my eye swept the buildings to the right, where the shots—if they really were shots; and it seemed unbelievable—might have come, I saw no significant sign of activity.

Four cars ahead, in the President's Continental limousine, a man in the front seat rose for a moment. He seemed to have a telephone in hand as he waved to a police cruiser ahead to go on.

The Presidential car leaped ahead and those following it attained breakneck speed as the caravan roared through

1. This area is the so-called grassy knoll, from which conspiracists claim at least one shot was fired.

the underpass and on to a broad freeway, police sirens whining shrilly. These sirens had been silenced by Presidential order throughout Mr. Kennedy's Texas trip.

Up to the highway we thundered, careening around a turn into the Parkland Hospital and screeching to a stop at the emergency entrance.

As we piled out of our car, I saw Mrs. Kennedy, weeping, trying to hold her husband's head up. Mrs. John Connally was helping hold up the Governor of Texas.

President in Back Seat

Mr. Connally's suit front was splattered with blood, his head rolling backward.

By the time I had covered the distance to the Presidential car, Secret Service men were helping Mrs. Kennedy away. Hospital attendants were aiding Mr. and Mrs. Connally.

For an instant I stopped and stared into the back seat. There, face down, stretched out at full length, lay the President, motionless.

His natty business suit seemed hardly rumpled. But there was blood on the floor.

"Is he dead?" I asked a Secret Service man.

"I don't know," he said, "but I don't think so."

I ran for a telephone.

A few minutes later I was back for more information.

The President and Mr. Connally had been moved into an emergency operating room. Vice President Johnson, Mrs. Johnson and Mrs. Kennedy had been escorted into the hospital.

The shiny White House automobile, a manufacturer's dream, stood untouched. It had been flown 1,500 miles from Washington only to become the death vehicle of the President, to whom it was designed to give maximum protection.

On the front seat floor lay the soft felt hat the President often carried but seldom wore. Beside it in mute comradeship was the wide-brimmed, light-colored Texas-style hat that Mr. Connally wore.

In the wide area between the seats, now cleared of its jump

seats, three twisted and torn roses lay in a pool of blood on the floor. Beside them was a tattered bouquet of asters.

It all seemed so unreal. This was the conveyance for what had been in the nature of triumph for Mr. Kennedy and the First Lady, who had been smiling, shaking hands and filled with happiness at a day of meeting the folks in the streets, the airports and the hotels.

Ironically, if their reception in Texas had not been so warm, precautions might have been taken to raise the shatter-proof side glasses even though the top of the convertible was down. Such protection might have saved the President.

But Dallas, where the President's policies had raised a storm of conservative protests, had been warm in its welcome to the handsome, bronzed President and his pretty, chic wife.

The Presidential party appeared to be chatting gaily among themselves after they had left the crowds of downtown Dallas behind and their caravan had swung into a quiet area where admirers had not chosen to stand.

But there the assassin took his stand.

His three well-aimed shots plunged America and the world into grief.

NORMAN SIMILAS, CANADIAN BUSINESSMAN:

"I was in Dallas on a convention and I decided to snap a picture of the President as the motorcade rolled by.

"The crowds had thinned out just past an overpass near the Trade Mart, so I had a good position when the motorcade came by at about 8 miles an hour.

"Then I suddenly heard a sharp crack. The first thing that came to my mind was that someone was setting off firecrackers. I turned away from the President's car and looked back to where the noise seemed to come from.

Agent Draws Gun

"Then somebody—I don't know who it was—yelled: 'The President's been shot.'

"I swung back to look at the car. A Secret Service man ran up with his gun drawn. A policeman beside me drew his revolver and his eyes searched the crowd.

"Then another shot rang out and a third almost immediately on top of it.

"I was still staring at the car. The Secret Service man opened the car door and I saw the President slumped down to the floor and falling toward the pavement.

"Jackie Kennedy was sitting on the left side of the car and Governor Connally on the President's right.

"I could see a hole in the President's left temple and his head and hair were bathed in blood.

"The agent looked in and gasped: 'Oh, my God, he's dead.'"

ALAN SMITH, MIDDLE SCHOOL STUDENT:
"It made me weak. I felt like sitting down. It was horrible.

"I was standing on the curb watching the parade along Main Street. We were permitted to skip school, if we had a note from our parents, to watch it.

"The crowds were cheering, but all at once they changed to screaming. The car was about 10 feet from me when a bullet hit the President in his forehead. The bullets came from a window right over my head in the building in front of which my friends and I were standing.[2]

"Mr. Kennedy had a big wide smile. But when he was hit his face turned blank. There was no smile no frown—nothing. He fell down over Jackie's knees and didn't say anything.

"She stood up screaming, 'God, oh God, no.' There was blood all over her and everything. She tried to raise him up but he fell back over her."

2. the Texas School Book Depository Building

The Assassin Is Assassinated

Gladwyn Hill

Two days after President Kennedy was assassinated, his assassin was assassinated. Lee Harvey Oswald was shot and killed by Jack Ruby, a Dallas nightclub operator, as Oswald was being transferred from one jail to another. According to several people who knew Ruby well, he acted because he wanted to keep Mrs. Kennedy from having to return to Dallas to testify in Oswald's trial. A number of conspiracy theorists contend, however, that Ruby shot Oswald to keep him from talking about his accomplices in the shooting of the president.

Gladwyn Hill was a reporter who covered the Kennedy assassination for the *New York Times*. In this article, he outlines what was known about Oswald's shooting shortly after it happened. Hill hints at the possibility that either Ruby or the Dallas Police Department had been involved in the Kennedy assassination, as was later alleged by a number of conspiracy theorists.

As you read, consider the following questions:
1. According to this article, why did Ruby shoot Oswald? Does this reason seem convincing?
2. Does this article suggest that the Dallas Police Department may have played an active role in silencing Oswald, and therefore in the Kennedy assassination?

President Kennedy's assassin, Lee Harvey Oswald, was fatally shot by a Dallas night-club operator today as the police started to move him from the city jail to the county jail.

The shooting occurred in the basement of the municipal building at about 11:20 A.M. central standard time (12:20 P.M. New York time).

The assailant, Jack Rubenstein, known as Jack Ruby, lunged from a cluster of newsmen observing the transfer of Oswald from the jail to an armored truck.

Millions of viewers saw the shooting on television.

As the shot rang out, a police detective suddenly recognized Ruby and exclaimed: "Jack, you son of a bitch!"

A murder charge was filed against Ruby by Assistant District Attorney William F. Alexander. Justice of the Peace Pierce McBride ordered him held without bail.

Detectives Flank Him

Oswald was arrested Friday after Mr. Kennedy was shot dead while riding through Dallas in an open car. He was charged with murdering the President and a policeman who was shot a short time later while trying to question Oswald.

As the 24-year-old prisoner, flanked by two detectives, stepped onto a basement garage ramp, Ruby thrust a .38-caliber, snub-nose revolver into Oswald's left side and fired a single shot.

The 52-year-old night-club operator, an ardent admirer of President Kennedy and his family, was described as having been distraught.

[District Attorney Henry Wade said he understood that the police were looking into the possibility that Oswald had been slain to prevent him from talking, The Associated Press reported. Mr. Wade said that so far no connection between Oswald and Ruby had been established.]

Oswald slumped to the concrete paving, wordlessly clutching his side and writhing with pain.

Oswald apparently lost consciousness very quickly after the shooting. Whether he was at any point able to speak, if he wanted to, was not known.

The politically eccentric warehouse clerk was taken in a

police ambulance to the Parkland Hospital, where President Kennedy died Friday. He died in surgery at 1:07 P.M., less than two hours after the shooting. The exact time Oswald was shot was not definitely established.

Four plainclothes men, from a detail of about 50 police officers carrying out the transfer, pounced on Ruby as he fired the shot and overpowered him.

Ruby, who came to Dallas from Chicago 15 years ago, had a police record here listing six allegations of minor offenses. The disposition of five was not noted. A charge of liquor law violation was dismissed. Two of the entries, in July, 1953, and May, 1954, involved carrying concealed weapons.

The city police, working with the Secret Service and the Federal Bureau of Investigation, said last night that they had the case against Oswald "cinched."

After some 30 hours of intermittent interrogations and confrontations with scores of witnesses, Oswald was ordered transferred to the custody of the Dallas County sheriff.

This was preliminary to the planned presentation of the case, next Wednesday or the following Monday, to the county grand jury by District Attorney Wade.

The transfer involved a trip of about a mile from the uptown municipal building, where the Police Department and jail are. The route went down Main Street to the county jail, overlooking the spot where President Kennedy was killed and Gov. John B. Connally was wounded by shots from the book warehouse where Oswald worked.

A Change in Plans

The original plan had been for the sheriff to assume custody of Oswald at the city jail and handle the transfer. Late last night, for unspecified reasons, it was decided that the city police would move the prisoner.

Police Chief Jesse Curry declined to comment on suggestions that he had scheduled the transfer of Oswald at an unpropitious time because of pressure from news media.

Chief Curry announced about 9 o'clock last night that

the investigation had reached a point where Oswald's presence was no longer needed. He said that Oswald would be turned over to the county sheriff today.

Asked when this would take place, the chief said: "If you fellows are here by 10 A.M., you'll be early enough."

When newsmen assembled at the police administrative offices at 10 o'clock, Chief Curry commented: "We could have done this earlier if I hadn't given you fellows that 10 o'clock time."

Armored Van Used

This was generally construed as meaning that preparations for the transfer had been in readiness for some hours, rather than implying a complaint from the chief that the press had had any part in setting the time.

Chief Curry disclosed this morning that to thwart an attempt against Oswald, the trip was to be made in an armored van of the kind used to transfer money.

"We're not going to take any chances," he said. "Our squad cars are not bullet-proof. If somebody's going to try to do something, they wouldn't stop him."

A ramp dips through the basement garage of the municipal building running from Main Street to Commerce Street. Patrol wagons drive down the ramp and discharge prisoners at a basement booking office. The garage ceiling was too low for the armored car, so the van was backed up in the Commerce Street portal of the ramp.

The plan was to lead Oswald out the doorway in the center of the basement and about 75 feet up the ramp to the back of the armored car.

Prisoner on Fourth Floor

At about 11 o'clock, Chief Curry left his third-floor office, followed by plainclothes detectives and newsmen, to go to the basement. Oswald was still in a fourth-floor jail cell.

As the group with the chief walked through a short corridor past the basement booking office and out the door onto the guarded ramp, uniformed policemen checked the reporters' credentials. But they passed familiar faces, such as those of policemen and collaborating Secret Service and F.B.I. agents.

Ruby's face was familiar to many policemen who had encountered him at his two night clubs and in his frequent visits in the municipal building.

Inconspicuous in Group

Neatly dressed in a dark suit and wearing a fedora, he was inconspicuous in a group of perhaps 50 men who for the next 20 minutes waited in a 12-foot-wide vestibule and adjacent portions of the ramp.

Television cameras facing the vestibule were set up against a metal railing separating the 15-foot-wide ramp from the rest of the garage. Some newsmen clustered along this railing.

Across Commerce Street, in front of a row of bail bondsmen's offices, a crowd of several hundred persons was held back by a police line.

Soon Oswald was taken in an elevator to the basement. He was led through the booking office to the open vestibule between two lines of detectives.

Walks Behind Captain

Captain Fritz, chief of the police homicide division, walked just ahead of him. Oswald was handcuffed, with a detective holding each arm and another following. On Oswald's right, in a light suit, was J.R. Leavelle and on his left, in a dark suit, L.C. Graves.

As they turned right from the vestibule to start up the ramp, Ruby jumped forward from against the railing. There was a sudden loud noise that sounded like the explosion of a photographer's flashbulb. It was Ruby's revolver firing.

A momentary furor set in as Ruby was seized and hustled into the building. Policemen ran up the ramp in both directions to the street, followed by others with orders to seal off the building.

About five minutes elapsed before an ambulance could be rolled down the ramp to Oswald.

The ambulance, its siren sounding, was followed by police and press cars on the four-mile drive to the hospital.

The hospital's emergency department had been on the alert for possible injuries arising out of the projected transfer.

Two days after Kennedy's assassination, Jack Ruby fatally shot Lee Harvey Oswald. Many Americans witnessed the shooting on television.

Oswald was moved almost immediately into an operating room, at the other end of the building from the one where President Kennedy was treated.

The bullet had entered Oswald's body just below his heart and had torn into most of the vital organs.

Dr. Tom Shires, the hospital's chief of surgery, who operated on Governor Connally Friday, took over the case. The gamut of emergency procedures—blood transfusion, fluid transfusion, breathing tube and chest drainage tube—was instituted immediately.

But Dr. Shires quickly reported through a hospital official that Oswald was in "extremely critical condition" and that surgery would take several hours.

Family Put in Custody

Oswald's brother, George, a factory worker from Denton, Tex. got to the hospital before the assassin died.

The police took Oswald's mother, wife and two infant daughters into protective custody. They were escorted to the hospital to view the body, then were taken to an undisclosed lodging place in Dallas.

Governor Connally is still a patient at the Parkland Hospital. The excitement of the Oswald case swirled around the temporary office the Governor had set up there.

Back at the jail, Ruby was taken to the same fourth-floor cellblock where his victim had been the focus of attention the past two days.

Reports that filtered out about his preliminary remarks said that he had been impelled to kill President Kennedy's assassin by sympathy for Mrs. Kennedy. It was reported he did not want her to go through the ordeal of returning to Dallas for the trial of Oswald.

District Attorney Wade said yesterday he was sure the prosecution of Oswald could be carried out without the personal involvement of any members of the Kennedy's family.

A half-dozen lawyers who have worked for Ruby converged on police headquarters in the next hour or two.

They said they had been directed there by relatives and friends of Ruby and had not been called by Ruby himself.

One lawyer said that he had arranged for a hearing before a justice of the peace tomorrow morning to ask for Ruby's release on bail.

"He's a respectable citizen who's been here for years and certainly is entitled to bail," the lawyer said. "We'll make any amount of bail."

"He is a great admirer of President Kennedy," the lawyer said, "and police officers."

The last remark was an allusion to the fact that Oswald was accused of fatally shooting the Dallas patrolman after the President's assassination.

Ruby, the lawyer, said, "is a very emotional man."

Chief Curry called the second formal news conference of the last three days at the police headquarters basement assembly room at 1:30 P.M.

His face drawn, he said in a husky voice:

"My statement will be very brief. Oswald expired at 1:07 P.M."

"We have arrested the man. He will be charged with murder. The suspect is Jack Rubenstein. He also goes by the name of Jack Ruby. That's all I have to say."

Sheriff Bill Decker commented that the police "did everything humanly possible" to protect Oswald, as he said they had in the case of President Kennedy.

"I don't think it would have made a bit of difference if Oswald had been transferred at night," he said. "If someone is determined to commit murder, it's almost impossible to stop him."

Ironically, it appeared that Ruby might have had a number of far easier opportunities for killing Oswald than the method he finally used.

He was reported to have circulated repeatedly the last two days among the throng of people that was constantly in the third-floor corridor near the homicide bureau. Oswald was led along this corridor a number of times as he was taken down from the fourth-floor jail for interrogation.

2

THE NATION AND THE WORLD RESPOND

CHAPTER PREFACE

Americans were stunned by the news of their leader's death. The charismatic Kennedy had been the nation's youngest president. He and his extended family were perhaps the closest thing in the eyes of many to being American royalty, certainly in terms of glamour and prestige. At the time, the nation was riding a wave of unprecedented economic prosperity, but Kennedy's death jolted many Americans out of their sense of well-being. A typical reaction was that of the New York Stock Exchange, which closed almost immediately upon hearing the news, the first time such a thing had ever happened. Many Americans were so shaken by Kennedy's death that, one year after the assassination, they were still grieving their fallen president.

Despite the good economic times, the assassination was symbolic of the violent times in which Americans were also living. The nation was embroiled in a Cold War with the Soviet Union and its Communist allies around the world, most notably Fidel Castro's Cuba. At the same time, the civil rights movement was polarizing a number of people, especially in the South, and many peaceful protest marches were marred by violence. This contentious spirit of the times led many Americans to wonder if, in some way, the nation as a whole had been responsible for Kennedy's death.

While Americans mourned their loss, people around the world also mourned. Kennedy had established himself in the minds of many, especially in Europe, as their champion. These people believed that under his leadership the United States would do everything in its power to protect the free world from being taken over by creeping communism. His successor, Lyndon Johnson, lacked Kennedy's credentials as a Cold War "warrior," and many people around the world worried that Kennedy's death might mean that the United States would be less interested in protecting freedom and capitalism than it had been during Kennedy's watch.

Even Communists had reason to mourn Kennedy's death. Fidel Castro of Cuba had become Kennedy's most bitter enemy, although by 1963 he and Kennedy were beginning to develop a grudging respect for each other. Castro feared that Americans would jump to the conclusion that he was at the center of a conspiracy to kill the president. This fear became more of a reality after it was disclosed that Lee Harvey Oswald, the primary suspect in Kennedy's death, had pro-Castro leanings.

Americans Mourn Their Fallen President

Tom Wicker

President Kennedy was perhaps the best-loved American president of all time. His youthful good looks, masterful oratory, and self-deprecating sense of humor endeared him to millions, in the United States and abroad, while his tough stance against the global spread of communism gave Americans a sense of security. His death came as a profound shock to people around the world, but especially to Americans. Like Pearl Harbor and the terrorist attacks on September 11, 2001, the Kennedy assassination represented a loss of innocence for an entire generation of American citizens.

In this article, Tom Wicker, a reporter for the *New York Times*, describes the scene along Pennsylvania Avenue in Washington, D.C., while Kennedy's coffin was taken from the White House to the Rotunda of the Capitol Building, where it lay in state. It also describes the surreal scene at the Rotunda, where hordes of Americans felt compelled to go pay their last respects to their slain leader.

As you read, consider the following questions:
1. Why were people willing to stand in line for hours and hours to spend only a few seconds gazing at the president's coffin?
2. What does the reaction of an unidentified woman to the news of Oswald's murder suggest about the American people's willingness to believe that a conspiracy was behind the president's death?

3. Do Chief Justice Earl Warren's remarks at the memorial service for Kennedy foreshadow the findings of the Warren Commission?

Thousands of sorrowing Americans filed past John Fitzgerald Kennedy's bier in the Great Rotunda of the United States Capitol yesterday and early today.

Mr. Kennedy's body lay in state in the center of the vast, stone-floored chamber. Long after midnight the silent procession of mourners continued.

Some wept. All were hushed. As the two lines moved in a large circle around either side of the flag-covered coffin, almost the only sounds were the shuffle of feet and the quiet voices of policemen urging the people to "keep moving, keep moving right along."

By 2:45 A.M. today 115,000 persons had passed the bier.

Yesterday afternoon a crowd estimated at 300,000 lined Pennsylvania and Constitution Avenues to watch the passage of the caisson bearing the body of the 35th President of the United States, slain in the 47th year of his life by an assassin's bullet.

A Riderless Horse

Behind the caisson, following military tradition, came a riderless bay gelding, with a pair of military boots reversed in the silver stirrups.

The horse was Sardar, the thoroughbred that belongs to Mrs. John F. Kennedy. Mrs. Kennedy, her two children, President and Mrs. Johnson and Mr. Kennedy's brother, Attorney General Robert F. Kennedy rode in the first car of a 10-car procession that followed the caisson.

The procession moved at a funeral pace, to the sound of muffled drums, from the White House to Pennsylvania Avenue. It was a journey Mr. Kennedy had made formally four times.

At the Capitol, brief ceremonies of eulogy were held in the Rotunda before the admission of the waiting thousands who swarmed over the plaza and stretched in a long line up East Capitol Street.

At the conclusion of the ceremonies, Mrs. Kennedy and her daughter, Caroline, stepped a few feet forward. Each reached out and touched the flag and the coffin it covered.

Mrs. Kennedy knelt, kissed the coffin, then rose and led her daughter away.

President Johnson had already come forward, following a soldier who walked backward carrying a wreath of red and white carnations. As the soldier placed the wreath at the foot of the coffin, the man who had taken Mr. Kennedy's place in office stood with his head bowed, then withdrew.

The wreath was marked "From President Johnson and the Nation." Numbers of other wreaths and sprays, sent despite a White House request that flowers be omitted, were arranged in nearby rooms.

After a short interval, during which staff workers of the Senate and the House of Representatives and their guests were admitted to the Rotunda from the North and South Wings of the Capitol, the great central doors of the Capitol were thrown open to the people.

Across the East Plaza, in long, silent lines, they came—patient, quiet, thousands upon thousands of them. They moved slowly up the towering marble steps, above which, on Jan. 20, 1961, a platform had been built for the Inaugural of John F. Kennedy as President of the United States.

As they entered the Rotunda, they formed two lines, each moving in a great semicircle around the Rotunda. Only red velvet ropes and 25 feet of stone floor separated them from the catafalque upon which rested Mr. Kennedy's coffin.

Enlisted men from each of the armed services stood motionless at the four corners of the catafalque. As the guard changed every half hour, first an Army officer, then a Marine Corps officer, then an officer from the Navy and the Air Force took up his position at the head of the coffin. They rotated command of the guard through the night.

Behind the commander, a sailor held the flag of the President. To the sailor's right stood an unattended American flag.

Footprints on Catafalque

Yesterday afternoon the dusty footprints of the military men who had placed the coffin upon the catafalque were still visible on the catafalque's black velvet drapings. At each side of the coffin were sprays of chrysanthemums and white lilies.

That simple scene was all the people saw as they filed past—the coffin covered with its flag, the motionless guards, the two listless flags upon their standards, the traditional flowers of death.

The police were nearly overwhelmed by a crowd far beyond their expectations. Within the Rotunda, however, all was order and silence. The lines moved rapidly around the circle—about 35 persons a minute in each line—and were directed out the west door to the wide porch that overlooks the Mall and the Washington Monument.

Outside, virtually the whole Metropolitan police force was on duty. At 4:30 P.M. the lines of those waiting to get in the Capitol stretched across the East Plaza back and six blocks, past the Supreme Court building on East Capitol Street.

At 9 P.M. the waiting line stretched for 30 blocks, with four to six persons abreast. And the line was growing, as people joined it faster than it moved through the Rotunda.

Thousands Turn Back

Originally, it had been planned to close the Capitol's doors at 9 P.M., reopening the Rotunda for an hour this morning. When the size of the crowds became apparent, it was decided to keep it open as long as people came.

Thousands were giving up late yesterday, however, under the impression that the doors would be closed by the time they reached the Rotunda. Families from as far away as Baltimore and Richmond left without having gotten near the Capitol.

However, millions throughout the county were watching on television. The brilliant lights needed for the cameras played steadily on the Rotunda and broadcasters spoke constantly in low monotones into their microphones. Across the wide lawns and the paved drives of the Capitol Plaza, the people coming and going swarmed like ants. Most were good-natured. There was little pushing and shoving, and no fighting was observed. But confusion was constant as people tried to find out where to get into line, how long it was and how to get out of the jammed plaza.

Even Mrs. Kennedy was inconvenienced by the crowds in the plaza. When she left the Capitol in a limousine with her children and Attorney General Kennedy, her planned route along Independence Avenue was impassable. She was rerouted over other streets, led by a motorcycle escort.

Throughout yesterday among the throngs that watched the procession and those that jammed around the Capitol, there were few evidences of open emotionalism. Not many people wept, or cried out. The mood was rather one of sorrow and respect.

Even among teen-agers, of whom thousands and thousands seemed to be present, there was quiet. People passing through the Rotunda were told that no photographs were to be taken; only a few, looking somewhat furtive, broke the restriction.

The police said some persons began lining up at midnight Saturday. Yesterday morning, hours before the procession began, crowds began to form along the streets and in Lafayette Square across Pennsylvania Avenue from the White House.

A half-hour before the procession began, the news reached the White House that Lee H. Oswald, charged with the murder of Mr. Kennedy in Dallas on Friday, had been shot down in that city.

Among the crowds many had transistor radios, and the news from Dallas swept rapidly. It was a constant subject of conversation in the crowd, and one gray-haired woman, seated on a bench in Lafayette Square, told her husband:

"I told you last night, Henry, I had a feeling something like this would happen. That man held so many secrets, some one had to kill him."

Another woman exclaimed: "My God, how long will this go on?"

On the lawn before the north portico of the White House, a small crowd of White House employees and workers in the Executive Office Building was permitted to assemble. The circular drive in front of the mansion was lined, shortly after noon, with black limousines. Near the northeast gate, an honor guard and the bearers of flags of all the states were lined up.

At 12:40 P.M., President and Mrs. Johnson arrived at the north portico and entered the black-draped doors of the building that will now be their home. Shortly thereafter, the empty caisson, draped in black and drawn by six gray horses, came up the drive and stopped under the portico.

It was the same caisson upon which the body of Franklin D. Roosevelt was carried from the White House to the Capitol in 1945.

Behind it was Sardar. The horse was given to Mrs. Kennedy in March, 1962, by President Ayub Khan of Pakistan when she visited that country. The White House said Mrs. Kennedy had requested that the horse be used as the traditional symbol of a fallen warrior. A black-handled sword hung in a silver scabbard from the saddle.

Mrs. Kennedy has ridden the horse in the hunt country around nearby Atoka, Va., where the late President built a new home.

The other horses were Army stock from Fort Myer in Virginia.

Then Mr. Kennedy's military aides, Maj. Gen. Chester V. Clifton of the Army, Brig. Gen. Godfrey McHugh of the Air Force and Capt. Tazewell T. Shepard Jr. of the Navy, lined up at attention behind the caisson.

Eight enlisted men of the various armed services carried the coffin out onto the north portico, down the few steps and placed it on the caisson. The military aides moved to the front. The caisson pulled slowly away, followed by the black horse. And a limousine slid into place at the foot of the steps.

Mrs. Kennedy, in black and wearing a black mantilla, came out holding Caroline and John Jr. by the hand. The children were dressed in identical shades of blue. The three entered the car and 2-year-old John Jr., apparently unaware of the nature of the occasion, bounced up on the seat and peered out the rear window.

Attorney General Kennedy followed them into the car. President and Mrs. Johnson took the jump seats, and the limousine pulled away.

In rapid order, other limousines drove up to the steps and were filled. In the second car were Mr. Kennedy's sisters Patricia and Jean, and their husbands, Peter Lawford and Stephen E. Smith. In the third were Mrs. Kennedy's stepfather and mother, Mr. and Mrs. Hugh D. Auchincloss, and others of the Auchincloss family.

Mrs. Robert Kennedy, several of her children, and Sargent Shriver, the husband of the former Eunice Kennedy, were in the next car. Mrs. Shriver, her mother, Mrs. Rose Kennedy, and Senator Edward M. Kennedy, the youngest brother, were flying to Washington from Hyannis Port, Mass., and were not in the procession.

A number of employees of the Kennedy family and the White House rode in another car.

Other cars with officials, security agents and policemen joined the line. As the procession moved slowly onto Pennsylvania Avenue, turned briefly on 15th Street, and then rounded on to the long straight stretch of Pennsylvania that reaches from the Treasury Building to the Capitol, the line was about two city blocks long.

Joint Chiefs March

In advance of the caisson, on foot, were policemen, the escort commander—Maj. Gen. Philip C. Wehle of the Military District of Washington—five military drummers, a drum major and a company of Navy enlisted men. They walked at funeral pace, 100 paces a minute. Behind them was a special honor guard, composed of the Joint Chiefs of Staff led by their chairman, Gen. Maxwell D. Taylor, and followed by Mr. Kennedy's military aides.

The national colors immediately preceded the caisson. Between it and the car carrying Mrs. Kennedy and President Johnson, there were personal flags, the marching body bearers, and the riderless Sardar.

Three clergymen also marched in the procession. They were the Very Rev. Francis Bowes Sayre Jr., dean of the Cathedral of Saints Peter and Paul (Washington Cathedral), Protestant Episcopal; the Right Rev. John S. Spencer of Sacred Heart Shrine (Roman Catholic); and the Very Rev. K.V. Kazanjian, rector of St. Mary's Armenian Apostolic Church. . . .

Crowds lined the entire route at least 10 deep and twice that thick at some places. Others stretched up the side streets, hung from windows of buildings along the street, lined open-tiered parking buildings and mounted the pedestals of the street's numerous statues.

At 25-foot intervals, soldiers with fixed bayonets lined the street on each side, standing at parade rest.

The Secret Service and the police, nervous after the Dallas motorcade that ended in death for Mr. Kennedy, took unusually stringent security precautions for Mr. Johnson.

As the President's car passed 14th Street, for instance, a police official was designating an officer to watch each building on the street. It was from a building beside a Dallas street that Mr. Kennedy was shot through the head by a sniper with a high-powered rifle.

For the first few blocks, the crowds stood silently, almost unmoving, as each element of the procession passed. As at the Capitol later, there were few evidences of emotionalism—very little, for instance, of the weeping, screaming and kneeling in the street that was observed at the last such occasion, the funeral procession for President Franklin Roosevelt 18 years ago.

A sizable group of reporters and photographers were allowed to walk in the street at the rear of the procession. Many of them had followed Mr. Kennedy in happier times when he drove to the Capitol along the same route for his inauguration, for two addresses to Congress in 1961, and for his State of the Union Messages in 1962 and 1963.

But their presence at the rear of the procession had been apparently mistaken by the crowd as an invitation for others to join. By the time the rear of the procession passed 11th Street, hundreds were seeping out from the curbs to walk behind Mr. Kennedy's coffin. Many were teen-agers, and some surged past the reporters as if to walk beside the cars ahead.

At Ninth Street, apparently on orders from a Secret Service car that pulled out of the procession, the police formed a cordon across the avenue and stopped the crowd which was massed from curb to curb and extended back for more than a block.

The reporters were let through the line at that point and continued along the avenue. Again, however, the crowds began coming from the curbside to join in. Finally, at John Marshall Place, a few blocks from the point where the procession slanted off onto Constitution Avenue, a line of marines with fixed bayonets halted everyone, including the reporters.

As the procession moved slowly up Capitol Hill on Constitution Avenue, and turned into the East Plaza, the restrictions were relaxed.

As seen from below, the sloping hillsides around the building were almost solidly covered with moving figures—many with children in their arms, some running, some leaping stone walls, all swarming up the hillside and the steps toward the West Front of the Capitol.

The police estimated that on the other side of the building, 35,000 persons were in the East Plaza to see the procession arrive.

The caisson and the cars following reached the east steps of the Capitol at 1:50 P.M., 45 minutes after the coffin had been borne from the White House. A 21-gun salute boomed across the crowd and echoed across the vast plaza stretching north to Union Station.

A military band played "Hail to the Chief." As the eight bearers removed the coffin from the caisson and bore it slowly up the marble steps, the band softly played—perhaps in honor of the service during which Mr. Kennedy nearly gave his life in World War II—the Navy hymn, "Eternal Father, Strong to Save."

The various parties from the limousines followed the coffin in the order they had arrived. Inside the Rotunda, members of the Senate, House and Cabinet and other dignitaries stood in a semicircle. Mrs. Kennedy, President and Mrs. Johnson and others who had come in the procession stood in the northeast quadrant of the hushed chamber, near a temporary lectern.

The members of the Kennedy family gathered near them. Caroline and John Jr. stood holding their mother's hands, Caroline sedately, John occasionally capering about.

Among those in the Rotunda was former President Harry S. Truman. He was accompanied by his daughter, Mrs. E.C. Daniel of New York.

Senator Mike Mansfield of Montana, the Democratic leader of the Senate, was the first eulogist.

Mansfield's Eulogy

As television lights washed the Rotunda in a harsh, artificial glare, Senator Mansfield spoke in tones that grew ever more ringing.

Four times, in praising the man who was dead, and the life he had lived for his country and with his wife, Senator Mansfield repeated:

"In a moment, it was no more. And so she took a ring from her finger and placed it in his hands."

A fifth time he said it and added—"and kissed him, and closed the lid of a coffin."

The Senator referred to Mrs. Kennedy's having put her ring on a finger of the President and having kissed him as the body was about to be taken to the plane for its return to Washington.

At that moment, the Senator said, "a piece of each of us died."

Mr. Kennedy, he said, "gave us of his love that we, too, in turn, might give. He gave that we might give of ourselves, that we might give to one another until there would be no room, no room at all, for the bigotry, the hatred, the prejudice and the arrogance which converged in that moment of horror to strike him down."

Chief Justice Earl Warren struck much the same note in the eulogy that followed.

"What moved some misguided wretch to do this horrible deed may never be known to us," he said, "but we do know that such acts are commonly stimulated by forces of hatred and malevolence, such as today, and are eating their way into the bloodstream of American life."

"What a price we pay for this fanaticism!" he declared.

Then the Chief Justice said:

"If we really love this country, if we truly love justice and mercy, if we fervently want to make this nation better for those who are to follow us, we can at least abjure the hatred that consumes people, the false accusations that divide us and the bitterness that begets violence.

"Is it too much to hope that the martyrdom of our beloved President might even soften the hearts of those who would themselves recoil from assassination, but who do not shrink from spreading the venom which kindles thoughts of it in others?"

Speaker of the House John W. McCormack was more personal.

"As we gather here today, bowed in grief," he said, "the heartfelt sympathy of the members of the Congress and of our people are extended to Mrs. Jacqueline and to Ambassador and Mrs. Joseph P. Kennedy and their loved ones.

"Their deep grief," he went on, "is also self-shared by countless millions of persons throughout the world; considered a personal tragedy, as if one had lost a loved member of his own immediate family."

Most of these remarks were inaudible to many in the chamber, which was not designed for speeches. Even strong voices are lost in the vast open space that rises above the stone floor to the top of the Capitol Dome.

During the eulogies, Mrs. Kennedy stood with regal bearing, seeming to listen intently. Tears rolled down the face of Robert F. Kennedy. At the moment that Mrs. Kennedy walked forward and knelt by her husband's coffin, all who saw her were profoundly moved.

Then it was over. Mrs. Kennedy and her children walked slowly down the steps of the Capitol. President and Mrs. Johnson followed. At the foot of the steps, in the softer light of the afternoon, they talked for a few moments.

Mrs. Johnson held Mrs. Kennedy's hands as they spoke; once she leaned forward and placed her head near Mrs. Kennedy's. Then the President took Mrs. Kennedy's hand in one of his, patted it with the other. Mrs. Kennedy, her children and Robert Kennedy entered a car and sped away.

Mr. Johnson, headed for one of the important meetings that will constantly occupy him in coming days, entered another car with Secret Service men and a military aide. After him, alone with her driver and a security guard, rode the new First Lady.

Behind them, in the stillness of the Rotunda, they left the body of John Fitzgerald Kennedy upon the same catafalque on which had rested—98 years ago—the body of Abraham Lincoln, the first American President to be murdered. Gazing on the scene with silent stone eyes from beside the north entrance was a statue of James A. Garfield, the second President to fall before an assassin.

It was time, then, for the doors to be opened to those waiting outside.

Americans Feel Responsible for the Assassination

Vermont Royster

Kennedy's assassination and the shooting death of his alleged assassin, Oswald, seemed to be such monstrous acts that many people refused to believe that they could be blamed on only two crazed gunmen. In the days following the deaths of Kennedy and Oswald, a number of observers remarked publicly that evil forces seemed to be at work. Several of these observers hinted that these forces were responsible for the two deaths and that they had been unleashed by the current condition of American society, which seemed to be turning increasingly violent and intolerant.

Vermont Royster was the editor of the *Wall Street Journal*, America's most respected business daily. He rejected the notion that any other than Oswald and Ruby were responsible for the terrible deeds surrounding Kennedy's death. In this article, an editorial written by Royster, he calls to task those American leaders who have suggested that Americans as a nation were somehow responsible for their president's death.

As you read, consider the following questions:
1. On whom or what does Royster place the blame for Kennedy's death?
2. Do you think that Royster thought that Kennedy was killed as a result of a conspiracy? If so, why? If not, why not?

In the shock of these past few days it is understandable that Americans should find their grief mingled with some shame that these events should happen in their country. We all stand a little less tall than we did last Friday morning.

Yet, for our own part, we find past understanding the remarks of some otherwise thoughtful men who, in their moment of shock, would indict a whole nation with a collective guilt. It seems to us that they themselves have yielded to the hysteria they would charge to others, and, in so doing, show that their own country is past their understanding.

Anyone who has been reading the newspapers, listening to the radio or watching television has heard these men— they include public commentators, members of our Congress and men of God. And the substance of what they charge is that the whole of the American people—and, by inclusion, the ways of the American society—are wrapped in a collective guilt for the murder of a President and the murder of a murderer.

A Senator said that the responsibility lay on "the people of Dallas" because this is where the events took place. A spokesman for one group of our people said the nation was "reaping the whirlwind of hatred." One of our highest judges said the President's murder was stimulated by the "hatred and malevolence" that are "eating their way into the bloodstream of American life." A newspaper of great renown passed judgment that "none of us can escape a share of the fault for the spiral of violence." And these were but a few among many.

Such statements can only come from men who have not been abroad in the land, neither paused to reflect how the events came about nor observed in what manner the whole American people have responded to tragedy.

A President lies dead because he moved freely among the people. He did so because he was beloved by many people, respected by all, and because everywhere people turned out in great numbers to pay him honor. In a society of tyranny the heads of state move in constant fear of murder, cor-

The assassination of Kennedy left Americans stunned. Groups of people gather at the White House in disbelief upon hearing the news of Kennedy's death.

doned behind an army of policemen. It is the fundamental orderliness of the American society that leads Presidents to move exposed to all the people, making possible the act of a madman.

In the tragedy there is blame, surely, for negligence. In retrospect, perhaps, it was negligent of a President himself not to be aware that there are ever madmen in the world; yet it is a negligence born of courage and confidence. It was negligent of the police authorities, perhaps, not to search and cover every corner, every window, which might shield a madman; yet it was a negligence born of years of proven trust in the crowds of Americans through which Presidents have safely moved.

It was most certainly a terrible negligence on the part of

the local police authorities which permitted one man to take vengeance into his own hands. It was an outrageous breach of responsibility for them to have moved a man accused of so heinous a crime in so careless a fashion. It was outrageous precisely because all the American people were themselves so outraged by the crime of assassination that anyone who knew these people ought to have known that one among them might be deranged enough to do exactly what was done.

Yet the opportunity for negligence came because here the accused was being treated as any other accused, his detention in the hands of local police, the procedures those followed for the most ordinary of murders. In another land he would have been efficiently buried by a secret police in a Lubyanka Prison, never again to be seen or heard of until his execution.

One might say, we suppose, that some of this negligence could be laid to all of us. It is, after all, the eager interest of the people in the persons of their leaders that brings them into open caravans, and it is the desire of the people to follow the normal ways even in murders of state that left the accused to bungling local police.

In sum, there is in all of this—let there be no mistake—much to grieve, to regret, to blame. We can't escape remorse that there are madmen in our midst, that a President is dead, that we have been denied the right to show in open court the virtue of a free society. Now we pay the price of all sorts of negligence.

But this is something different from the charge in the indictment. It is more than nonsense to say that the good people of Dallas, crowding the streets to honor a President, share a murderous guilt; or that the tragic acts of madmen cast a shadow on the whole of America. Such an indictment is vicious.

Of reasons for shame we have enough this day without adding to them a shameful injustice to a mourning people.

People Around the World Mourn Kennedy's Death

Time

People around the world loved President Kennedy. Africans and Latin Americans loved him because he promised to treat them as equal partners rather than as second-class citizens. Most Western Europeans thought highly of him because he opposed communism in the Soviet Union and promised to stop its spread. Many Asians thought similarly, as Kennedy also opposed the spread of communism from China. To most of the so-called free world, Kennedy represented America's commitment to political and economic freedom; for many, he personified American idealism and strength. Even his enemies in the Soviet Union and Cuba respected him because of his straightforward ways. His death set off a wave of international mourning that was unprecedented in the annals of history.

Seven days after Kennedy's assassination, *Time* magazine examined the world's response to the president's death. This article presents the magazine's report.

As you read, consider the following questions:
1. Does the world's response to Kennedy's death seem a bit bizarre? Would the world react the same way today to the death of an American president? If so, why? If not, why not?
2. What do the responses of Nikita Khrushchev and Fidel Castro suggest about possible Soviet or Cuban involvement in Kennedy's assassination?

In halting English, a Moslem telegraph operator in the Middle East tapped out on the telex: "Is it correct Kennedy killed pls?" When New York replied, "Yes, an hour ago," the Moslem signed off, "How sorrowful bad."

As the shadow of the news spread across the world, it was received everywhere with stunned disbelief. The Empress of Iran broke into tears, as did the President of Tanganyika, and countless anonymous men and women. Along Rome's Via Veneto grief sounded operatic. "*E morto!*" people called to one another, and at a cocktail party the guests put down their glasses and began to recite the Lord's Prayer.

Wherever monarchs still ruled—in the United Kingdom, in Jordan—formal court mourning was proclaimed. Hardly a nation in the world failed to order the rites of tolling bells and lowered flags. Theaters and sports arenas closed down on individual impulse. With the news of Kennedy's death, a Viennese ice show halted in mid-performance; in Belgium, a six-day bicycle race was interrupted; in distant Nepal, the ceremonial opening of a leprosarium was postponed.

Everywhere, bars, cafés and restaurants emptied long before closing time. Strangers spoke to each other in short, simple phrases—"Poor Jackie," or "How awful," or "It can't be true." The phones of Americans abroad never ceased ringing, as foreign friends and acquaintances—or even total strangers—called to offer sympathy. The streets in front of U.S. embassies were jammed with mourners who stood in line for hours to write their names in books of condolence. Some brought flowers, but many searched out an American diplomat merely to shake his hand.

Monstrous Act

One by one the statesmen joined the chorus of commiseration. As Big Ben tolled every minute for one hour (a gesture normally reserved for deaths in the royal family), Prime Minister Sir Alec Douglas-Home said: "There are times when the mind and the heart stand still." From Sir Winston Churchill came a statement: "This monstrous act has taken from us a great statesman and a wise and valiant man." The words still seemed to carry the old, sibilant indignation of the ancient lion. Liberia's President William Tubman cabled: "The urn of grief has been opened and is being filled with the tears of friends the world over." Israel's David Ben-Gurion only asked: "Why, why?"

Almost by reflex, people rushed to disclaim even remote complicity in the murder. "Thank God it wasn't a Negro," said a Negro in Toronto. Many others insisted on reading into the event their own political passions. Statesmen in Africa, Asia and elsewhere insisted that the deed must have been done by a racist, and that Kennedy was a martyr like Lincoln or Gandhi. And Nehru could not resist remarking that the murder gave evidence of "dark corners in the U.S., and this great tragedy is a slap for the concept of democracy."

Golden Boy

The mourning voices first of all were for the President of the United States, regardless of his name or identity. For in a sense far beyond daily foreign policy squabbles, he is to much of the world the protector of the weak, the benefactor of the poor.

Because of the changes in the cold war climate that occurred during his Administration, millions, even on the enemy side, mourned John Kennedy as a man of peace. But above all they mourned him for his person. Perhaps even more than his own countrymen, other peoples saw in him the embodiment of American virtues—youth, strength, informality, good looks, the idealistic belief that all problems can eventually be solved. A Southern Rhodesian paper called him "the golden boy," and Common Market President Walter Hallstein said that Kennedy "personified the most beautiful qualities of his people."

Possibly more than any other President in U.S. history, he had set out to charm the world, and he had succeeded in convincing many a nation that it was his special favorite.

Alive, John Kennedy had been particularly idolized by the citizens of West Germany, who received him last June as they had no other foreign leader. When the President told a crowd of 150,000 West Berliners, *"Ich bin ein Berliner,"*[1] the German people were his. Dead, John Kennedy was instantly enshrined by Germans as a hero. On the night of his assassination, 25,000 West Berlin students assembled and marched on city hall, where Mayor Willy Brandt, exhausted from a trip to Africa, told them: "I know how many are weeping tonight. We Berliners are poorer tonight. We all have lost one of the best."

West Germany's Chancellor Ludwig Erhard was on his special train returning from a Paris meeting with Charles de Gaulle. A Scotch and soda at his elbow, he was briefing himself for a trip to Washington to see Kennedy, scheduled for this week. When Erhard's press chief came suddenly into the car and burted out the news that Kennedy was dead, Erhard sat in a stunned silence. Finally he murmured, *"Unfassbar, kaum fassbar* [Inconceivable, hardly conceivable]."

Under Fire

In Paris, the news reached President de Gaulle in his private apartment at the Elysée Palace. He turned on his TV set. When Kennedy's death was confirmed, De Gaulle—himself twice the target of assassination attempts—called in his staff. His face drawn and pale, he dictated his statement of condolence: "President Kennedy has died like a soldier, under fire. . . ." Russia's Red Army Choir, performing at Paris' Palais des Sports, interrupted its program for the announcement of the death and then, after a moment of silence, sang a Schubert *lied* in Kennedy's memory.

In Geneva, Swiss citizens jammed traffic by abandoning their cars in the middle of the streets to snatch up newspapers. An old woman, tears staining her cheeks, cried, "What an age we are living in!"

In Spain, no foreigner has ever won the public's heart as

---

1. "I am a Berliner," meaning that Kennedy would protect West Berlin, at the time a Western enclave in the midst of Communist East Germany, from being taken over by Communists

had Kennedy. Said a Madrid editor, "Nothing has jolted me so much since the start of our own Civil War." Americans were sought out for a pat on the shoulder, a comforting phrase such as, "*Hombre, lo siento mucho* [Man, I feel deeply]."

Italy was locked in a political crisis when the news came. Premier Aldo Moro promptly adjourned his attempts to form a Cabinet with left-wing Socialist Leader Pietro Nenni. Emerging from the meeting, 72-year-old Nenni, with tears in his eyes, said: "These are little affairs of ours, in the face of this tragedy for the whole world." At the Vatican Pope Paul went to his private chapel to pray for the wounded President and, after the news of his death, said Mass.

To Ireland, John Kennedy was the apotheosis of the country's hopes and history—the great-grandson of a poor immigrant who had stormed the ramparts of the New World and won its highest honor. He was looked upon, said the Irish Times, "as a younger brother and with great affection."

Reichstag Fire

On the other side of the Iron Curtain, Chairman Nikita Khrushchev and two aides drove to the U.S. embassy in Moscow. Dressed in black and looking noticeably depressed, Khrushchev spoke for 19 minutes with U.S. Ambassador Foy Kohler, reminiscing about the slain President. Khruschev's wife Nina cabled Jacqueline Kennedy. The genuine dismay in Russia was soon modified by politics, when it turned out that the prime suspect was a self-declared Marxist who had lived in Russia. Said one Soviet journalist suspiciously: "Is this affair being whipped up in the press? Is the situation grim?" Said another Russian taking up what sounded like an emerging propaganda line: "Remember that they found a Communist who started the Reichstag fire."[2]

---

2. The Reichstag fire was one event that led to Adolf Hitler's taking control of Germany. It was set by Nazis, who then blamed it on the Communists.

In the Middle East, one Iraqi was amazed: "We are used to this kind of thing in Arab countries. But in America?" In the Congo, East Katanga's President Edouard Bulundwe and his entire Cabinet, together with their seldom seen wives, trooped into the home of the U.S. consul. "This is how we behave in Africa when a great chief dies," explained Bulundwe as they sat stiffly in the drawing room. "President Kennedy will be mourned in even the smallest village of our country as a man who cared for and worked for the blacks."

It was the same in Asia. In Thailand, authorities sent sound trucks into the villages to spread the mournful news that *Prathanathibodi* (President) Kennedy was dead. In Saigon, people were more shocked by Kennedy's death than they had been by that of President Diem; and Buddhists held special memorial services and prayers. In Japan, technicians were up before dawn to receive the historic first trans-Pacific TV broadcast from the U.S., which was to have included a personal message from the President. Instead, the voice of a Japanese newsman in Manhattan reported the news of Kennedy's death.

In all of Asia, Red China was almost alone in its determined lack of sympathy. Peking radio carried the Kennedy story without comment. The Hong Kong Communist New Evening Post sneered that Kennedy had "used a two-faced policy to promote an imperialist war course."

Vanishing Baiters

Even Cuba proved less surly than Red China. Fidel Castro deplored the murder, said he had no reason to wish for Kennedy's death, but conceded that "perhaps" Cuba might have had motives "to feel like it" and vaguely suggested that "reactionaries" were really to blame. Elsewhere in Latin America, all the Yankee baiting seemed to disappear for the moment. A sense of pessimism about the future gripped Brazil, and the downtown streets of Rio de Janeiro were filled with people whose tight faces, glazed eyes and unaccustomed silence revealed their feelings. In the *favelas* (shantytowns) on Rio's outskirts, samba bands called off their rehearsals for the carnival, and President João Goulart said about Kennedy: "I kneel before his memory."

The most eloquent Latin American voices were those heard in the street. A janitor in Quito, who had been listening to the news on radio, refused to read his newspaper because "it's too painful to go over such a sad story again." Despite later revelations about the crime, most Latin Americans persisted in believing that Kennedy had been slain because of his support for Negro rights. In Buenos Aires, women cried, *"Qué barbaridad!"*, and old men made sad, futile gestures with their hands. Said one grieving Colombian: "It seems as though all the Presidents in all the Latin American countries have died."

To the north, throughout Canada, theaters and arenas closed their doors, and large cities became hushed with a curious quiet. Prime Minister Lester Pearson was just about to open a session of Parliament when he was handed a note. He threw it on the top of his desk, slumped back in his seat and seemed at a loss for words. His voice broke as he said: "The world can ill afford at this time in our history to lose a man of his courage."

History's more precise appraisals would come later, as would the resumption of all the world's usual enmities. But for a brief time at least, the U.N. General Assembly, standing in silence, was in a mood to agree with U.S. Ambassador Adlai Stevenson, who said: "All of us who knew him will bear the grief of his death to the day of ours."

"Assassination Is Repellent to Me"

Fidel Castro and Jean Daniel

At the time of Kennedy's death, Fidel Castro had been the leader of Cuba for four years. During that period, he and Kennedy became bitter enemies, mostly because the United States was actively working to stamp out communism in Cuba, and with it Castro's regime. It was a well-known fact that the two men did not like each other; it was later disclosed that the CIA had tried to assassinate Castro on eight different occasions, and it seemed likely to many Americans that Castro wished nothing better than to see Kennedy dead. Consequently, many conspiracy theorists are convinced that Castro was the mastermind behind Kennedy's assassination.

Jean Daniel was a French journalist who happened to be interviewing Castro at the exact moment that Castro was told about Kennedy's death. In this article, he describes Castro's reaction to the news from the United States, first of the assassination and later that Oswald was believed to be some sort of Cuban agent.

As you read, consider the following questions:
1. What do Castro's remarks to Daniel on November 19 and his initial reaction to the news of Kennedy's death suggest about Castro's role in the assassination?
2. What do Castro's remarks to Daniel after the news of Kennedy's death suggest about Castro's role in the assassination?

It was around 1:30 in the afternoon, Cuban time. We were having lunch in the living room of the modest summer residence which Fidel Castro owns on magnificent Varadero Beach, 120 kilometers from Havana. For at least the tenth time, I was questioning the Cuban leader on details of the negotiations with Russia before the missile installations last year. The telephone rang, a secretary in guerrilla garb announced that Mr. Dorticós, President of the Cuban Republic, had an urgent communication for the Prime Minister. Fidel picked up the phone and I heard him say: *"Como? Un atentado?"* ("What's that? An attempted assassination?") He then turned to us to say that Kennedy had just been struck down in Dallas. Then he went back to the telephone and exclaimed in a loud voice *"Herido? Muy gravemente?"* ("Wounded? Very seriously?")

Castro Gets Bad News

He came back, sat down, and repeated three times the words: *"Es una mala noticia."* ("This is bad news.") He remained silent for a moment, awaiting another call with further news. He remarked while we waited that there was an alarmingly sizable lunatic fringe in American society and that this deed could equally well have been the work of a madman or of a terrorist. Perhaps a Vietnamese? Or a member of the Ku Klux Klan? The second call came through: it was hoped they would be able to announce that the United States President was still alive, that there was hope of saving him. Fidel Castro's immediate reaction was: "If they can, he is already re-elected." He pronounced these words with satisfaction.

This sentence was a sequel to a conversation we had held on a previous evening and which had turned into an all-night session. To be precise, it lasted from 10 in the evening until 4 in the morning. A good part of the talk revolved about the impressions I recounted to him of an interview which President Kennedy granted me this last October 24, and about Fidel Castro's reactions to these impressions.

During this nocturnal discussion, Castro had delivered himself of a relentless indictment of US policy, adding that in the recent past Washington had had ample opportunity to normalize its relations with Cuba, but that instead it had tolerated a CIA program of training, equipping and organizing a counter-revolution. He had told me that he wasn't in the least fearful of his life, since danger was his natural milieu, and if he were to become a victim of the United States this would simply enhance his radius of influence in Latin America as well as throughout the socialist world. He was speaking, he said, from the viewpoint of the interests of peace in both the American continents. To achieve this goal, a leader would have to arise in the United States capable of understanding the explosive realities of Latin America and of meeting them halfway. Then, suddenly, he had taken a less hostile tack: "Kennedy could still be this man. He still has the possibility of becoming, in the eyes of history, the greatest President of the United States, the leader who may at last understand that there can be coexistence between capitalists and socialists, even in the Americas. He would then be an even greater President than Lincoln. I know, for example, that for Khrushchev, Kennedy is a man you can talk with. I have gotten this impression from all my conversations with Khrushchev. Other leaders have assured me that to attain this goal, we must first await his re-election. Personally, I consider him responsible for everything, but I will say this: he has come to understand many things over the past few months; and then too, in the last analysis, I'm convinced that anyone else would be worse." Then Fidel had added with a broad and boyish grin: "If you see him again, you can tell him that I'm willing to declare Goldwater my friend if that will guarantee Kennedy's re-election!"

This conversation was held on November 19.

Now it was nearly 2 o'clock and we got up from the table and settled ourselves in front of a radio. Commandant Vallero, his physician, aide-de-camp, and intimate friend, was easily able to get the broadcasts from the NBC network in Miami. As the news came in, Vallero would translate it for Fidel: Kennedy wounded in the head; pursuit of the assassin; murder of a policeman; finally the fatal announcement: President Kennedy is dead. Then Fidel stood up and said to me: "Everything is changed. Everything is going to change. The United States occupies such a position in world affairs that the death of a President of that country affects millions of people in every corner of the globe. The cold war, relations with Russia, Latin America, Cuba, the Negro question . . . all will have to be rethought. I'll tell you one thing: at least Kennedy was an enemy to whom we had become accustomed. This is a serious matter, an extremely serious matter."

After the quarter-hour of silence observed by all the American radio stations, we once more tuned in on Miami, the silence had only been broken by a re-broadcasting of the American national anthem. Strange indeed was the impression made, on hearing this hymn ring out in the house of Fidel Castro, in the midst of a circle of worried faces. "Now," Fidel said, "they will have to find the assassin quickly, but very quickly, otherwise, you watch and see, I know them, they will try to put the blame on us for this thing. But tell me, how many Presidents have been assassinated? Four? This is most disturbing! In Cuba, only one has been assassinated. You know, when we were hiding out in the Sierra there were some (not in my group, in another) who wanted to kill Batista.[1] They thought they could do away with a regime by decapitating it. I have always been violently opposed to such methods. First of all from the viewpoint of political self-interest, because so far as Cuba is concerned, if Batista had been killed he would have been replaced by some military figure who would have tried to make the revolutionists pay for the martyrdom of the dictator. But I was also opposed to it on personal grounds; assassination is repellent to me."

The broadcasts were now resumed. One reporter felt he

---

1. Fulgencio Batista, the Cuban dictator who was deposed by Castro

should mention the difficulty Mrs. Kennedy was having in getting rid of her bloodstained stockings. Fidel exploded: "What sort of a mind is this!" He repeated the remark several times: "What sort of a mind is this? There is a difference in our civilizations after all. Are you like this in Europe? For us Latin Americans, death is a sacred matter; not only does it mark the close of hostilities, but it also imposes decency, dignity, respect. There are even street urchins who behave like kings in the face of death. Incidentally, this reminds me of something else: if you write all those things I told you yesterday against Kennedy's policy, don't use his name now; speak instead of the policy of the United States government."

Toward 5 o'clock, Fidel Castro declared that since there was nothing we could do to alter the tragedy, we must try to put our time to good use in spite of it. He wanted to accompany me in person on a visit to a *granja de pueblo* (state farm), where he had been engaging in some experiments. His present obsession is agriculture. He reads nothing but agronomical studies and reports. He dwells lyrically on the soil, fertilizers, and the possibilities which will give Cuba enough sugar cane by 1970 to achieve economic independence.

"Didn't I Tell You"

We went by car, with the radio on. The Dallas police were now hot on the trail of the assassin. He is a Russian spy, says the news commentator. Five minutes later, correction: he is a spy married to a Russian. Fidel said: "There, didn't I tell you; it'll be my turn next." But not yet. The next word was: the assassin is a Marxist deserter. Then the word came through, in effect, that the assassin was a young man who was a member of the "Fair Play for Cuba Committee," that he was an admirer of Fidel Castro. Fidel declared: "If they had had proof, they would have said he was an agent, an accomplice, a hired killer. In saying simply that he is an admirer, this is just to try and make an association in people's minds between the name of Castro and the emotion awakened by the assassination. This is a publicity method, a propaganda device. It's terrible. But you know, I'm sure this will all soon blow over. There are too many competing policies in the United States for any single one to be able to impose itself universally for very long."

We arrived at the *granja de pueblo*, where the farmers welcomed Fidel. At that very moment, a speaker announced over the radio that it was now known that the assassin is a "pro-Castro Marxist." One commentator followed another; the remarks became increasingly emotional, increasingly aggressive. Fidel then excused himself: "We shall have to give up the visit to the farm." We went on toward Matanzas from where he could telephone President Dorticós. On the way he had questions: "Who is Lyndon Johnson? What is his reputation? What were his relations with Kennedy? With Khrushchev? What was his position at the time of the attempted invasion of Cuba?" Finally and most important of all: "What authority does he exercise over the CIA?" Then abruptly he looked at his watch, saw that it would be half an hour before we reached Matanzas and, practically on the spot, he dropped off to sleep.

After Matanzas, where he must have decreed a state of alert, we returned to Varadero for dinner. Quoting the words spoken to him by a woman shortly before, he said to me that it was an irony of history for the Cubans, in the situation to which they had been reduced by the blockade, to have to mourn the death of a President of the United States. "After all," he added, "there are perhaps some people in the world to whom this news is cause for rejoicing. The South Vietnamese guerrillas, for example, and also, I would imagine, Madame Nhu!"[2]

I thought of the people of Cuba, accustomed to the sight of posters like the one depicting the Red Army with maquis[3] superimposed in front, and the screaming captions

2. Madame Nhu was the sister-in-law of the president of South Vietnam and the government's official hostess, in essence the First Lady. After her husband, the head of South Vietnam's secret police, was killed in a U.S.-backed coup, she took up residence in the United States. 3. members of an underground resistance movement

"HALT, MR. KENNEDY! CUBA IS NOT ALONE. . . ."
I thought of all those who had been led to associate their deprivations with the policies of President John F. Kennedy. At dinner I was able to take up all my questions. What had motivated Castro to endanger the peace of the world with the missiles in Cuba? How dependent was Cuba on the Soviet Union? Is it not possible to envisage relations between Cuba and the United States along the same lines as those between Finland and the Russians? How was the transition made from the humanism of Sierra Maestra to the Marxism-Leninism of 1961? Fidel Castro, once more in top form, had an explanation for everything. Then he questioned me once more on Kennedy, and each time I eulogized the intellectual qualities of the assassinated President, I awakened the keenest interest in him.

The Cubans have lived with the United States in that cruel intimacy so familiar to me of the colonized with their colonizers. Nevertheless, it was an intimacy. In that very seductive city of Havana to which we returned in the evening, where the luminous signboards with Marxist slogans have replaced the Coca Cola and toothpaste billboards, in the midst of Soviet exhibits and Czechoslovakian trucks, a certain American emotion vibrated in the atmosphere, compounded of resentment, of concern, of anxiety, yet also, in spite of everything, of a mysterious almost imperceptible rapprochement. After all, this American President was able to reach accord with our Russian friends during his lifetime, said a young Cuban intellectual to me as I was taking my leave. It was almost as though he were apologizing for not rejoicing at the assassination.

One Year Later, the Nation Still Mourns

Time

Kennedy's death bothered a great many Americans for years after it happened. On the first anniversary of his death, more than one-third of all Americans said they felt worse, not better, while another one-third said they felt no better. To help them handle their grief, people resorted to a number of things to commemorate his life. Their actions made it clear that, one year later, the Kennedy assassination was one of the most traumatic events in the history of the nation.

On November 27, 1964, *Time* magazine featured a number of articles that focused on Kennedy, his legacy, and the legacy of his passing. In this article, the anonymous author describes some of the things people felt compelled to do to honor the dead president. The author also touches briefly upon the lives of several people who were connected in an important way to the assassination.

As you read, consider the following questions:
1. Why did Americans still have trouble getting over Kennedy's death a year later?
2. Based on this article, what would you say the nation lost when Kennedy died?
3. What does Jack Ruby's behavior, as outlined in this article, suggest about his possible role in either the assassination or its cover-up?

The tributes to John F. Kennedy's memory poured forth, ranging from official orations to folk songs, from churchly ritual to crass commercialism, from public breast beating to silent prayer. It was the anniversary of the assassination, and those who knew his quick, sensitive, critical mind could not help but speculate on how he would have commented on the observance.

The "Broody" Look

In Washington, President Johnson issued a proclamation saying: "In churches and homes everywhere, on Nov. 22 let us rededicate ourselves to the pursuit of the ideals of human dignity in which he believed and whose course he so brilliantly illuminated." A shop-window placard in New York's Times Square proclaimed SALE! COLLECTOR'S ITEM. KENNEDY HALF-DOLLAR. 88¢. Boston's Richard Cardinal Cushing prepared a sermon for a special Mass that said: "He became the voice of mankind to interpret the issues of the day and to help lead our generation to higher levels toward an era of relaxing tension, human hopes, and peace on earth. We thank God, however, that we had him, even for less than three years, as the first Catholic President of the United States." And an NBC-TV producer named Lou Hazam spoke boastfully about his Kennedy documentary (one of several commemorative efforts by networks) because his crew had shot the route of Kennedy's funeral procession in infra-red film: "It turns the sky black, the leaves on the trees white, and we get a 'broody' look."

Lou Harris, Kennedy's favorite pollster in 1960, reported on a national survey indicating that 35% of the people miss Kennedy more now than they did a year ago, that 35% have no strong feelings, and that 30% believe that "time is healing the wound." Nearly five-dozen books about Kennedy or his assassination are on the market. West Germany proudly issued a new J.F.K. postage stamp last week, but tiny Sierra Leone had already achieved an insurmountable lead in that category by printing 14 different Kennedy stamps in the last year. A bronze bust of Kennedy by Sculptor Felix de Weldon, who did the massive statue of the Iwo Jima flag raising for the Marine Corps War Memorial in Arlington, Va., was accepted by President Johnson; it will eventually be placed in the $10 million Kennedy Memorial Library.

Gaucherie & Tears

A special memorial symphony was written by Roy Harris (an American composer frequently given to writing symphonic paeans to the U.S.) for performance by the Royal Philharmonic Orchestra in London. The University of Indiana chorus prepared a new oratorio, taken from a Nov. 24, 1963, New York Times editorial that began: "The leaden skies of yesterday were like a pall." Sicilian troubadours chanted a musical legend that grew up among the island's villagers after Kennedy died: "With his big heart and full of courage/ He attracted the people with his manner/ And many, many learned the language/ Of peace and loyalty without making fools of themselves."

The U.S. Information Agency last week issued for public showing in 114 countries (but not the U.S.) a 90-minute documentary film, narrated by Gregory Peck, called *John F. Kennedy: Years of Lightning, Day of Drums*. Among selected U.S. audiences who were allowed to see the film, some persons who had been close to Kennedy felt that it reflected too much Hollywood gaucherie. But to most it brought unabashed tears.

At Kennedy's tomb in Arlington National Cemetery, where a $2,000,000 monument is planned, thousands marched by each day. Cemetery authorities had received so many requests to lay wreaths at the graveside on Nov. 22 that they closed reservations months ago, granted permission for 21 such ceremonies; among the privileged few were West German Foreign Minister Gerhard Schröder and Juanita Castro, anti-Castro sister of the Cuban dictator. Last week Miss Castro said that her brother was in part responsible for Kennedy's assassination because he "must have influenced" Lee Oswald by constantly calling the President "the illiterate millionaire" and a "murderer."

The family planned no special observance. Mother Rose

and Father Joe were to stay at Hyannis Port. Jackie, as her official year of mourning came to an end, planned to remain pretty much in seclusion. Bobby was to attend Mass in Washington's St. Matthew's Cathedral, where the President's funeral was held. Teddy is still hospitalized, but was about to take his first steps since his back was broken in June, and now hopes to walk under his own power into the Senate when it convenes in January.

"Essence of Potentiality"

The outpouring of memorials was new testimony to the well-established fact that John F. Kennedy's style had caught the imagination of people around the world.

The best of the memorials were, correctly, a tribute to his spirit rather than an attempt to overstate his accomplishments. Amid all the words written or spoken or sung, none put the tragedy and the truth of Kennedy's death into better perspective than the first two sentences in the script of *An Essay on Death*, a National Education Television documentary. "This is a program about death. It is also a commemoration of a man who was among us a short while ago, and one who, having been the essence of potentiality, stirred in us a deep and perplexing grief because that potentiality was shattered in an instant."

The Others

And what of some of the other people drawn, whether or not by their own design, into the assassination of President Kennedy and its aftermath? In the intervening year, the lives of most of them have changed dramatically.

Marina Oswald, 23, the assassin's Russian-born wife, was a pitiable creature, beaten and burdened by a psychotic husband who was a flat-out failure in every way. After Oswald was killed, sympathetic people sent Marina some $60,000. She moved into a $15,000, three-bedroom, air-conditioned brick house in a Dallas suburb. She had her teeth fixed, now affects fashionable coiffures and Neiman-Marcus clothes. She bought her own membership in Dallas' Music Box, a private club, and she turns up frequently with dates. Marina tosses down shots of vodka, chases them with 7-Up. She often outdrinks her escorts, despite the fact that when Oswald was alive he forbade her to drink hard liquor. She chain-smokes, though Oswald once slapped her for smoking a cigarette in his presence. So far, she has refuse to change her name, although she worries some about the stigma affecting her children, June Lee, 2, and Rachel, 1. She has had mountains of marriage proposals and other bizarre propositions (a man from Kentucky offered her $50,000 if she would let him exhibit Oswald's body in a sideshow, another $100,000 if she would accompany the display). She still broods about last Nov. 22, and she feels particularly bad about Jackie Kennedy's loss. "It's hard enough to lose a bad husband," said Marina. "I wonder how it is to lose a good one." As the assassination anniversary rushed at her last week, Marina Oswald became increasingly tense and morose. At week's end she checked

President Kennedy was immensely popular with the public. His assassination is one of the most traumatic events in the nation's history.

into a hospital. The cause: nervous exhaustion.

Jack Ruby, 53, the strip-joint owner who killed Oswald in the Dallas police station, often kneels in beady-eyed terror on the floor of his jail cell, and babbles that he can hear the screams of U.S. Jews who are being killed or castrated in the streets because of his crime. Such are his demented dreams that previously friendly guards have all but stopped playing dominoes with him, and Ruby spends hours hunched over on his bunk playing solitaire. Ruby has tried three times to kill himself—by battering his head against a wall, ripping up his trousers to make a noose, and poking his finger in an electric light socket. Ruby's onetime pride and joy, the tawdry Carousel Club, has been sold, and Mrs. Grant [a family friend] says the family is nearly broke. Ruby's attorney, Phil Burleson, last week filed a 6,341-page appeal and transcript of Ruby's trial in hopes that the state Court of Criminal Appeals would grant another hearing— possibly in February or March.

Marguerite Oswald, 57, the assassin's mother, lives in Fort Worth and wallows in woe and self-pity. She still insists shrilly that her son did not murder Kennedy alone, says: "I think Lee was a patsy. I think President Kennedy was a victim of people in the State Department." She complains that she has been taken by money-grabbing writers who gleaned information from her, then "didn't even send me $10." She asks, "Why shouldn't there be as much sympathy for me as the President's family? After all, my son was murdered." Mrs. Oswald frequently visits her son's grave in Fort Worth's Rose Hill Cemetery, sometimes lays bouquets of plastic flowers at the headstone. Fort Worth police still maintain an all-night guard at the gravesite to prevent vandalism.

Mrs. J.D. Tippit, 36, wife of the Dallas policeman Oswald killed, received sympathy contributions totaling $643,863.08. She has spent almost none of the money, still lives in the same modest house in a Dallas suburb (a Philadelphia banker has paid off the mortgage), has the same 1961 station wagon (which still has generator trouble). Half of her fortune is in trust for her two sons, 14 and 5, and her daughter, 11. In the dining room of her home there is a photograph of the Kennedy family, with an inscription from Jackie Kennedy saying: "There is another bond we share. We must remind our children all the time what brave men their fathers were."

Governor John Connally, 47, who was wounded in the same limousine in which Kennedy died, was uneasy in large crowds during his winning gubernatorial campaign this fall, often jumped nervously at sudden noises. His right wrist, smashed with one of Oswald's bullets, still gives him trouble. He must eat left-handed, has difficulty brushing his teeth, cannot handle small coins with his right hand. Obviously scarred by his involvement, he sobbed recently during a television interview about the assassination. At a press conference last week, he said: "More than ever before, I have tried to keep uppermost in my mind what things are of lasting value and to be grateful for the time I have, to be more aware of the things you really hold dear and to be constantly grateful for the things you really know in your heart to be of lasting value and strength."

Jesse Curry, 51, chief of the Dallas Police Department, drew volcanic criticism for allowing reporters and cameramen at police headquarters to all but dictate his handling of Oswald and for setting up security standards so lax that it was easy for Ruby to shoot Oswald while the U.S. watched on television. Curry suffers from high blood pressure, seldom appears in public now, but his job is considered safe, for if Dallas officials fired him they would be in effect admitting the city's responsibility for the shameful affair.

3

THE WARREN COMMISSION REPORT AND ITS SUPPORTERS

CHAPTER PREFACE

One week after taking office, President Lyndon Johnson ordered a complete investigation into the Kennedy assassination. Johnson appointed a presidential commission, headed by Chief Justice Earl Warren, to conduct the investigation. The Warren Commission, as it became known, was charged with determining who had shot Kennedy and why.

The Warren Commission interviewed many of the people who had witnessed the murder in Dealey Plaza as well as a number of people who had known either Lee Harvey Oswald or Jack Ruby. It also examined reams of documents provided by the FBI, which served as the commission's investigative arm. In September 1964, less than ten months after it had begun its work, the commission issued a final report. Its conclusion was that Oswald had acted alone in shooting the president, and that Ruby had acted alone in shooting Oswald.

Given the controversy that later arose over the commission's findings, many Americans are surprised to learn that *The Warren Commission Report* received high marks from a good many eminent judges, law professors, and legal historians. All agreed that the report did not answer every question concerning Kennedy's death and that some questions might never be answered. Nevertheless, most legal experts agreed that the commission had done the best it could, given what it had to work with. They also generally agreed that, of all the possible scenarios that had been advanced to explain who had killed Kennedy and why, the commission's version made the most sense.

All Shots Were Fired from the Texas School Book Depository Building

The Warren Commission

The gunshots that rang through Dealey Plaza on November 22, 1963, created such an echo that many witnesses were unsure of where the shots originated. Although a majority of the witnesses who heard the shots later testified that they seemed to come from the Texas School Book Depository Building from which they were allegedly fired by Oswald, a significant minority were convinced that they came from another location, specifically the grassy knoll, a landscaped hill between Dealey Plaza and the railroad bridge over the Triple Underpass. Some witnesses also claimed to have seen a puff of smoke coming from behind a stockade fence between the grassy knoll and the bridge, thus making the claim that shots were fired from this vicinity more convincing. In order to get to the bottom of the assassination, the Warren Commission felt compelled to determine conclusively the source of the shots.

This article is an excerpt from *The Warren Commission Report*'s chapter on the shots from the Texas School Book Depository Building. It presents the eyewitness testimony of several witnesses, as well as the results of a partial recreation of the assassination, in an effort to prove that the shots that killed the president were fired from that building and nowhere else.

As you read, consider the following questions:
1. Do you agree with the commission's conclusion that

The Warren Commission, *The Warren Commission Report: The Official Report of the President's Commission on the Assassination of President John F. Kennedy*. Stamford, CT: Longmeadow Press, 1992.

three shots were fired from the Texas School Book Depository Building? If so, why? If not, why not?

2. Do you agree with the commission's conclusion that no shots were fired from the railroad bridge or the grassy knoll? If so, why? If not, why not?

3. What do you make of Lee E. Bowers Jr.'s comment that, prior to the assassination, he found it difficult to distinguish between sounds coming from the vicinity of the Depository Building and sounds coming from the vicinity of the Triple Underpass, that is, the grassy knoll?

Passengers in the first few cars of the motorcade had the impression that the shots came from the rear and from the right, the general direction of the Texas School Book Depository Building, although none of these passengers saw anyone fire the shots. Some spectators at Houston and Elm Streets, however, did see a rifle being fired in the direction of the President's car from the easternmost window of the sixth floor on the south side of the building. Other witnesses saw a rifle in this window immediately after the assassination. Three employees of the Depository, observing the parade from the fifth floor, heard the shots fired from the floor immediately above them. No credible evidence suggests that the shots were fired from the railroad bridge over the Triple Underpass, the nearby railroad yards or any place other than the Texas School Book Depository Building.

Near the Depository

Eyewitnesses testified that they saw a man fire a weapon from the sixth-floor window. Howard L. Brennan, a 45-year-old steamfitter, watched the motorcade from a concrete retaining wall at the southwest corner of Elm and Houston, where he had a clear view of the south side of the Depository Building. (See Commission Exhibit No. 477, p. 62.)[1] He was

---

1. Exhibit #477 is a photograph of the Texas School Book Depository Building from where Brennan was standing.

approximately 107 feet from the Depository entrance and 120 feet from the southeast corner window of the sixth floor. Brennan's presence and vantage point are corroborated by a motion picture of the motorcade taken by amateur photographer Abraham Zapruder, which shows Brennan, wearing gray khaki work clothes and a gray work helmet, seated on the retaining wall. Brennan later identified himself in the Zapruder movie. While waiting about 7 minutes for the President to arrive, he observed the crowd on the street and the people at the windows of the Depository Building. He noticed a man at the southeast corner window of the sixth floor, and observed him leave the window "a couple of times."

Brennan watched the President's car as it turned the corner at Houston and Elm[2] and moved down the incline toward the Triple Underpass. Soon after the President's car passed, he heard an explosion like the backfire of a motorcycle. Brennan recalled:

> Well, then something, just right after this explosion, made me think that it was a firecracker being thrown from the Texas Book Store. And I glanced up. And this man that I saw previous was aiming for his last shot.

> Well, as it appeared to me he was standing up and resting against the left window sill, with gun shouldered to his right shoulder, holding the gun with his left hand and taking positive aim and fired his last shot. As I calculate a couple of seconds. He drew the gun back from the window as though he was drawing it back to his side and maybe paused for another second as though to assure hisself that he hit his mark, and then he disappeared.

Brennan stated that he saw 70 to 85 percent of the gun when it was fired and the body of the man from the waist up. The rifle was aimed southwesterly down Elm Street to-

2. The Depository stood at this corner.

ward the underpass. Brennan saw the man fire one shot and he remembered hearing a total of only two shots. When questioned about the number of shots, Brennan testified:

I don't know what made me think that there was fire-crackers throwed out of the Book Store unless I did hear the second shot, because I positively thought the first shot was a backfire, and subconsciously I must have heard a second shot, but I do not recall it. I could not swear to it.

Brennan quickly reported his observations to police officers. . . .

Amos Lee Euins, a 15-year-old ninth grade student, stated that he was facing the Depository as the motorcade turned the corner at Elm and Houston. He recalled:

Then I was standing here, and as the motorcade turned the corner, I was facing, looking dead at the building. And so I seen this pipe thing sticking out the window. I wasn't paying too much attention to it. Then when the first shot was fired, I started looking around, thinking it was a backfire. Everybody else started looking around. Then I looked up at the window, and he shot again.

After witnessing the first shots, Euins hid behind a fountain bench and saw the man shoot again from the window in the southeast corner of the Depository's sixth floor. According to Euins, the man had one hand on the barrel and the other on the trigger. Euins believed that there were four shots. Immediately after the assassination, he reported his observations to Sgt. D.V. Harkness of the Dallas Police Department and also to James Underwood of station KRLD-TV of Dallas. Sergeant Harkness testified that Euins told him that the shots came from the last window of the floor "under the ledge" on the side of the building they were facing. Based on Euins' statements, Harkness radioed to headquarters at 12:36 P.M. that "I have a witness that says that it came from the fifth floor of the Texas Book Depository Store." Euins accurately described the sixth floor as the floor "under the ledge." Harkness testified that the error in the radio message was due to his own "hasty count of the floors."

Other witnesses saw a rifle in the window after the shots were fired. Robert H. Jackson, staff photographer, Dallas Times Herald, was in a press car in the Presidential motorcade, eight or nine cars from the front. On Houston Street about halfway between Main and Elm, Jackson heard the first shot. As someone in the car commented that it sounded like a firecracker, Jackson heard two more shots. He testified:

> Then we realized or we thought that it was gunfire, and then we could not at that point see the President's car. We were still moving slowly, and after the third shot the second two shots seemed much closer together than the first shot, than they were to the first shot. Then after the last shot, I guess all of us were just looking all around and I just looked straight up ahead of me which would have been looking at the School Book Depository and I noticed two Negro men in a window straining to see directly above them, and my eyes followed right on up to the window above them and I saw the rifle or what looked like a rifle approximately half of the weapon, I guess I saw, and just as I looked at it, it was drawn fairly slowly back into the building, and I saw no one in the window with it.

> I didn't even see a form in the window.

In the car with Jackson were James Underwood, television station KRLD-TV; Thomas Dillard, chief photographer, Dallas Morning News; Malcolm O. Couch and James Darnell, television newsreel cameramen. Dillard, Underwood, and the driver were in the front seat, Couch and Darnell were sitting on top of the back seat of the convertible with Jackson. Dillard, Couch, and Underwood confirmed that Jackson spontaneously exclaimed that he saw a rifle in the window. According to Dillard, at the time the shots were fired he and his fellow passengers "had an absolutely perfect view of the School Depository from our position in the open car." Dillard immediately took two pictures of the building: one of the east two-thirds of the south side and the other of the southeast corner, particularly the fifth- and sixth-floor windows. These pictures show three Negro men in windows on the fifth floor and the partially open window on the sixth floor directly above them. (See Dillard Exhibits C and D, pp. 66–67.)[3] Couch also saw the rifle in the window, and testified:

And after the third shot, Bob Jackson, who was, as I recall, on my right, yelled something like, "Look up in the window! There's the rifle!"

And I remember glancing up to a window on the far right, which at the time impressed me as the sixth or seventh floor, and seeing about a foot of a rifle being— the barrel brought into the window.

Couch testified he saw people standing in other windows on the third or fourth floor in the middle of the south side, one of them being a Negro in a white T-shirt leaning out to look up at the windows above him.

Mayor and Mrs. Earle Cabell rode in the motorcade immediately behind the Vice-Presidential followup car. Mrs. Cabell was seated in the back seat behind the driver and was facing U.S. Representative Ray Roberts on her right as the car made the turn at Elm and Houston. In this position Mrs. Cabell "was actually facing" the seven-story Depository when the first shot rang out. She "jerked" her head up immediately and saw a "projection" in the first group of windows on a floor which she described both as the sixth floor and the

3. Exhibits C and D are photographs of the windows in question.

top floor. According to Mrs. Cabell, the object was "rather long looking," but she was unable to determine whether it was a mechanical object or a person's arm. She turned away from the window to tell her husband that the noise was a shot, and "just as I got the words out . . . the second two shots rang out." Mrs. Cabell did not look at the sixth-floor window when the second and third shots were fired.

James N. Crawford and Mary Ann Mitchell, two deputy district clerks for Dallas County, watched the motorcade at the southeast corner of Elm and Houston. After the President's car turned the corner, Crawford heard a loud report which he thought was backfire coming from the direction of the Triple Underpass. He heard a second shot seconds later, followed quickly by a third. At the third shot, he looked up and saw a "movement" in the far east corner of the sixth floor of the Depository, the only open window on that floor. He told Miss Mitchell "that if those were shots they came from that window." When asked to describe the movement more exactly, he said,

> . . . I would say that it was a profile, somewhat from the waist up, but it was a very quick movement and rather indistinct and it was very light colored. . . .

> When I saw it, I automatically in my mind came to the conclusion that it was a person having moved out of the window. . . .

He could not state whether the person was a man or a woman. Miss Mitchell confirmed that after the third shot Crawford told her, "Those shots came from that building." She saw Crawford pointing at a window but was not sure at which window he was pointing.

On the Fifth Floor
Three Depository employees shown in the picture taken by Dillard were on the fifth floor of the building when the shots were fired: James Jarman, Jr., age 34, a wrapper in the ship-

ping department; Bonnie Ray Williams, age 20, a ware-houseman temporarily assigned to laying a plywood floor on the sixth floor; and Harold Norman, age 26, an "order filler." Norman and Jarman decided to watch the parade during the lunch hour from the fifth-floor windows. From the ground floor they took the west elevator, which operates with push-button controls, to the fifth floor. Meanwhile, Williams had gone up to the sixth floor where he had been working and ate his lunch on the south side of that floor. Since he saw no one around when he finished his lunch, he started down on the east elevator, looking for company. He left behind his paper lunch sack, chicken bones and an empty pop bottle. Williams went down to the fifth floor, where he joined Norman and Jarman at approximately 12:20 P.M.

Harold Norman was in the fifth-floor window in the southeast corner, directly under the window where witnesses saw the rifle. (See Commission Exhibit No. 485, p. 69.)[4] He could see light through the ceiling cracks between the fifth and sixth floors. As the motorcade went by, Norman thought that the President was saluting with his right arm,

. . . and I can't remember what the exact time was but I know I heard a shot, and then after I heard the shot, well, it seems as though the President, you know, slumped or something, and then another shot and I believe Jarman or someone told me, he said, "I believe someone is shooting at the President," and I think I made a statement "It is someone shooting at the President, and I believe it came from up above us."

Well, I couldn't see at all during the time but I know I heard a third shot fired, and I could also hear something sounded like the shell hulls hitting the floor and the ejecting of the rifle. . . .

4. Exhibit #485 is a photograph of a re-creation of the assassination, showing the positions of the three Depository employees during the shooting.

Williams said that he "really did not pay any attention" to the first shot—

> . . . because I did not know what was happening. The second shot, it sounded like it was right in the building, the second and third shot. And it sounded—it even shook the building, the side we were on. Cement fell on my head.
>
> Q. You say cement fell on your head?
>
> A. Cement, gravel, dirt, or something, from the old building, because it shook the windows and everything. Harold was sitting next to me, and he said it came right from over our head.

Williams testified Norman said "I can even hear the shell being ejected from the gun hitting the floor."

When Jarman heard the first sound, he thought that it was either a backfire—

> . . . or an officer giving a salute to the President. And then at that time I didn't, you know, think too much about it. . . .
>
> Well, after the third shot was fired, I think I got up and I run over to Harold Norman and Bonnie Ray Williams, and told them, I said, I told them that it wasn't a backfire or anything, that somebody was shooting at the President.

Jarman testified that Norman said "that he thought the shots had come from above us, and I noticed that Bonnie Ray had a few debris in his head. It was sort of white stuff, or something." Jarman stated that Norman said "that he was sure that the shot came from inside the building because he had been used to guns and all that, and he said it didn't sound like it was too far off anyway." The three men ran to the west side of the building, where they could look toward the Triple Underpass to see what had happened to the motorcade.

After the men had gone to the window on the west side of the building, Jarman "got to thinking about all the debris on Bonnie Ray's head" and said, "That shot probably did come from upstairs, up over us." He testified that Norman said, "I know it did, because I could hear the action of the bolt, and I could hear the cartridges drop on the floor." After pausing for a few minutes, the three men ran downstairs. Norman and Jarman ran out of the front entrance of the building, where they saw Brennan, the construction worker who had seen the man in the window firing the gun, talking to a police officer, and they then reported their own experience.

On March 20, 1964, preceding their appearance before the Commission, these witnesses were interviewed in Dallas. At that time members of the Commission's legal staff conducted an experiment. Norman, Williams, and Jarman placed themselves at the windows of the fifth floor as they had been on November 22. A Secret Service agent operated the bolt of a rifle directly above them at the southeast corner window of the sixth floor. At the same time, three cartridge shells were dropped to the floor at intervals of about 3 seconds. According to Norman, the noise outside was less on the day of the assassination than on the day of the test. He testified, "Well, I heard the same sound, the sound similar. I heard three something that he dropped on the floor and then I could hear the rifle or whatever he had up there." The experiment with the shells and rifle was repeated for members of the Commission on May 9, 1964, on June 7, 1964, and again on September 6, 1964. All seven of the Commissioners clearly heard the shells drop to the floor.

At the Triple Underpass

In contrast to the testimony of the witnesses who heard and observed shots fired from the Depository, the Commission's investigation has disclosed no credible evidence that any shots were fired from anywhere else. When the shots were fired, many people near the Depository believed that the shots came from the railroad bridge over the Triple Underpass or from the area to the west of the Depository.[5] In the hectic moments after the assassination, many spectators ran in the general direction of the Triple Underpass or the railroad yards northwest of the building. Some were running toward the place from which the sound of the rifle fire appeared to come, others were fleeing the scene of the shooting. None of these people saw anyone with a rifle, and the Commission's inquiry has yielded no evidence that shots were fired from the bridge over the Triple Underpass or from the railroad yards.

On the day of the motorcade, Patrolman J.W. Foster stood on the east side of the railroad bridge over the Triple Underpass[6] and Patrolman J.C. White stood on the west side. Patrolman Joe E. Murphy was standing over Elm Street on the Stemmons Freeway overpass, west of the railroad bridge farther away from the Depository. Two other officers were stationed on Stemmons Freeway to control traffic as the motorcade entered the Freeway. Under the advance preparations worked out between the Secret Service and the Dallas Police Department, the policemen were under instructions to keep "unauthorized" people away from these locations. When the motorcade reached the intersection of Elm and Houston Streets, there were no spectators on Stemmons Freeway where Patrolman Murphy was stationed. Patrolman Foster estimated that there were 10 or 11 people on the railroad bridge where he was assigned; another witness testified that there were between 14 and 18 people there as the motorcade came into view. Investigation has disclosed 15 persons who were on the railroad bridge at this time, including 2 policemen, 2 employees of the Texas-Louisiana Freight Bureau and 11 employees of the Union Terminal Co. In the absence of

5. This area is the grassy knoll. As several witnesses testified, the grassy knoll and the area behind the fence were clearly visible to anyone standing on the bridge.
6. From this position, Foster was in a perfect position to see anything happening on the grassy knoll or behind the stockade fence.

any explicit definition of "unauthorized" persons, the policemen permitted these employees to remain on the railroad bridge to watch the motorcade. At the request of the policemen, S.M. Holland, signal supervisor for Union Terminal Co., came to the railroad bridge at about 11:45 A.M. and remained to identify those persons who were railroad employees. In addition, Patrolman Foster checked credentials to determine if persons seeking access to the bridge were railroad employees. Persons who were not railroad employees were ordered away, including one news photographer who wished only to take a picture of the motorcade.

Another employee of the Union Terminal Co., Lee E. Bowers, Jr., was at work in a railroad tower about 14 feet above the tracks to the north of the railroad bridge and northwest of the corner of Elm and Houston, approximately 50 yards from the back of the Depository. (See Commission Exhibit No. 2218, p. 73.)[7] From the tower he could view people moving in the railroad yards and at the rear of the Depository. According to Bowers, "Since approximately 10 o'clock in the morning traffic had been cut off into the area so that anyone moving around could actually be observed." During the 20 minutes prior to the arrival of the motorcade, Bowers noticed three automobiles which entered his immediate area; two left without discharging any passengers and the third was apparently on its way out when last observed by Bowers. Bowers observed only three or four people in the general area, as well as a few bystanders on the railroad bridge over the Triple Underpass.

As the motorcade proceeded toward the Triple Underpass, the spectators were clustered together along the east concrete wall of the railroad bridge facing the oncoming procession. (See Commission Exhibit No. 2215, p. 75.)[8] Patrolman Foster stood immediately behind them and could observe all of them. Secret Service agents in the lead car of the motorcade observed the bystanders and the po-

7. Exhibit #2218 is a map and two photographs showing the view from the railroad tower. 8. Exhibit #2215 is a map and photograph of the railroad bridge from the direction that the presidential motorcade approached it.

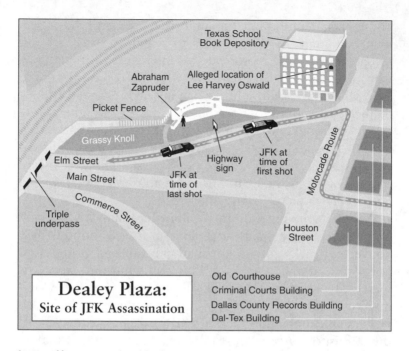

Dealey Plaza:
Site of JFK Assassination

Texas School
Book Depository

Abraham
Zapruder

Alleged location of
Lee Harvey Oswald

Picket Fence

Grassy Knoll

Elm Street

Main Street

Highway
sign

JFK at
time of
first shot

JFK at
time of
last shot

Motorcade Route

Commerce Street

Triple
underpass

Houston
Street

Old Courthouse
Criminal Courts Building
Dallas County Records Building
Dal-Tex Building

lice officer on the bridge. Special Agent Winston G. Lawson motioned through the windshield in an unsuccessful attempt to instruct Patrolman Foster to move the people away from their position directly over the path of the motorcade. Some distance away, on the Stemmons Freeway overpass above Elm Street, Patrolman Murphy also had the group on the railroad bridge within view. When he heard the shots, Foster rushed to the wall of the railroad bridge over the Triple Underpass and looked toward the street. After the third shot, Foster ran toward the Depository and shortly thereafter informed Inspector Herbert J. Sawyer of the Dallas Police Department that he thought the shots came from the vicinity of Elm and Houston.

Other witnesses on the railroad bridge had varying views concerning the source and number of the shots. Austin L. Miller, employed by the Texas-Louisiana Freight Bureau, heard three shots and thought that they came from the area of the Presidential limousine itself. One of his coworkers, Royce G. Skelton, thought he heard four shots, but could not tell their exact source. Frank E. Reilly, an electrician at Union Terminal, heard three shots which seemed to come from the trees "On the north side of Elm Street at the corner up there." According to S.M. Holland, there were four shots which sounded as though they came from the trees on the north side of Elm Street where he saw a puff of smoke. Thomas J. Murphy, a mail foreman at Union Terminal Co., heard two shots and said that they came from a spot just west of the Depository. In the railroad tower, Bowers heard three shots, which sounded as though they came either from the Depository Building or near the mouth of the Triple Underpass. Prior to November 22, 1963, Bowers had noted the similarity of the sounds coming from the vicinity of the Depository and those from the Triple Underpass, which he attributed to "a reverberation which takes place from either location."

Immediately after the shots were fired, neither the policemen nor the spectators on the railroad bridge over the Triple Underpass saw anything suspicious on the bridge in their vicinity. (See Commission Exhibit No. 2214, p. 74.)[9] No one saw anyone with a rifle. As he ran around through the railroad yards to the Depository, Patrolman Foster saw no suspicious activity. The same was true of the other bystanders, many of whom made an effort after the shooting to observe any unusual activity. Holland, for example, immediately after the shots, ran off the overpass to see if there was anyone behind the picket fence on the north side of Elm Street, but he did not see anyone among the parked cars. Miller did not see anyone running across the railroad tracks or on the plaza west of the Depository. Bowers and others saw a motorcycle officer dismount hurriedly and come running up the incline on the north side of Elm Street. The motorcycle officer, Clyde A. Haygood, saw no one running from the railroad yards.[10]

9. Exhibit #2214 is a map and photographs of the view from the railroad bridge looking toward Dealey Plaza.   10. In essence, Foster, Holland, Miller, Bowers, and Haygood saw no suspicious activity on the grassy knoll or in the area behind the stockade fence.

A Law Professor Praises
The Warren Commission Report

Herbert L. Packer

Most Americans have heard a great deal about *The Warren Commission Report*'s detractors, but few even know that the report won a great deal of praise from legal experts when it first came out. These experts examined the report as one would a prosecutor's case in a murder trial. Although they acknowledged that the report does not explain every single nagging detail or discrepancy, the vast majority of them concluded that it does establish Oswald's guilt beyond a reasonable doubt.

The reaction of Herbert L. Packer was typical of the legal experts who concurred in the Warren Commission's findings. Packer was a professor of law at Stanford University and the author of a book about the role of eyewitnesses as a fact-finding tool. In this article, an excerpt from an article Packer wrote for the *Nation*, he argues that the report makes a compelling case for its conclusion that Oswald acted alone.

As you read, consider the following questions:
1. Why does Packer accept the findings of the Warren Commission? Does his reasoning make sense to you? If so, why? If not, why not?
2. To what degree is Packer critical of *The Warren Commission Report*? Does this criticism seem reasonable to you? If so, why? If not, why not?

The Warren Commission has admirably fulfilled its central objective by producing an account of the circumstances under which President Kennedy was assassinated that is adequate to satisfy all reasonable doubts about the immediate, essential facts. We now know as much as we are ever likely to know about what happened in Dallas. Why it happened remains, perhaps forever, obscure. If there are minor flaws in the report—some unavoidable, others, as I shall suggest, that might have been corrected—they are thrown into shadow by the conscientious and at times brilliant job that the commission has done. Only those who for whatever reasons of personal or political myopia cannot bring themselves to face reality will continue to think that the tragedy was proximately the work of more than one man and therefore ultimately the outcome of a conspiracy. The fantasts will continue to differ about whose conspiracy it was—Texas oil millionaires or Kremlin operatives—but their central premise will continue to hold. The important difference is that now the supposed factual basis for their premise, as well as for more reasoned doubts about what appeared to be the truth, has been dissolved.

The commission's relations with the outside world during the period of its investigation have not been altogether fortunate. Regrettably, the difficulties have not ceased and must now affect any immediate judgment on their product. The problem during the investigatory period was one of too much information. There was a series of leaks, some unplanned, others bearing at least the appearance of calculation, that suggested the crystallizing of a "position" long before one could confidently have been arrived at. The most spectacular of these was the revelation, scant weeks after the commission was organized, that the FBI report confirmed the theory that Oswald, acting alone, was the assassin. That leak may well have been beyond the commission's control but, taken in conjunction with others that were not, it created an impression of prejudgment that could not help but detract from the confidence with which the findings would be received. It is the measure of the commission's achievement that qualms of this sort have been, at least in the immediate aftermath, muted. Whether they will continue to be so remains to be seen and will depend to a considerable extent on what happens when the new problem of too little information is rectified.

I refer to the fact that the supporting volumes of transcripts and exhibits, originally slated for release simultaneously with the report volume, are still not available and apparently will not be released for some weeks. This should not have been allowed to happen. Whether the fault lies with the commission or with the White House, it is a grievous one. What it means, very simply, is that there is not at this time an adequate basis for evaluating the quality of the commission's fact-finding process. The problem is particularly acute in the case of findings that rest wholly or largely on testimony by eyewitnesses. By a careful reading of the report one learns who some of these witnesses were and what the commission thought was established by their testimony. What one cannot learn is how their testimony was probed by the inquiry. Much of that process is doubtless contained in working papers that will never be published, but the public record of the commission will include a good deal of it. One assumes from the quality of the report that the probing was detailed and penetrating; but that remains a surmise until the raw material is available for examination.

It may well be that once the report was in the President's hands he had no alternative but to release it at once. If so, the commission should not have transmitted it until the supporting data could be made publicly available. That kind of reticence may have been rendered difficult by the apparent ease with which the press was able to learn how far along in its work the commission was. If so, it is sufficient answer that this body had unique reason to know that accommodating the press is not the *summum bonum*.[1]

---

1. *Summum bonum* is Latin for "the highest good." Packer refers to the fact that Jack Ruby was able to shoot Lee Harvey Oswald in part because the Dallas Police Department allowed the media to witness the transfer of Oswald from one jail to another.

Fortunately, the report and some of its appendices permit evaluation of the central findings. The factual controversies have been so numerous that it is easy to lose sight of the distinction between what is important and what is merely interesting. What is primarily important is the physical facts of the assassination. We now have as reliable evidence on that score as we are ever likely to get. That evidence fatally impairs the viability of the various conspiracy, or revisionist, theories that have been advanced in the months since the assassination. I do not propose to analyze the evidence in detail. Readers of this article have presumably read the report. (It should, but probably does not, go without saying that no one who has not read the report, and read it carefully as a whole, should feel himself entitled to hold an opinion about its virtues or defects.) What I shall do is separate out the central core of evidence that demonstrates beyond peradventure that one man, acting alone, fired all shots that were fired at the Presidential limousine and that the man was, beyond a reasonable doubt, Lee Harvey Oswald.

(1) *All of the wounds sustained by President Kennedy and by Governor Connally were inflicted by bullets fired from the rear and above.* This is demonstrated by the medical report on Governor Connally and the autopsy report on the President, as corroborated by (a) examination of the bullet holes in the President's clothing, which showed that the first shot that hit him entered his back and exited through the lower part of his neck; (b) the damage to the inside of the windshield caused by a spent bullet fragment; (c) the absence of any damage that could have been caused by a bullet or bullets fired from the front.

(2) *All of the shots were fired from the sixth-floor window of the Texas School Book Depository (TSBD).* This is demonstrated by (a) the re-enactment of the shooting accomplished with the aid of the motion picture of the actual shooting taken by Abraham Zapruder, which proved consistent with the medical and ballistics evidence with respect to the wounds; (b) the presence of three used cartridge

cases on the floor near the window from which the shots were hypothesized to have been fired; (c) the presence of a rifle on the same floor; (d) the absence of any bullets or bullet fragments not accounted for by the fire from the TSBD.

(3) *The shots were fired from the Mannlicher-Carcano rifle found on the sixth floor of the TSBD.* This is demonstrated by the results of the ballistic tests on the bullet and bullet fragments that were recovered, and on the cartridge cases found on the sixth floor of the TSBD.

(4) *Oswald was the owner of the rifle used in the assassination.* This is demonstrated by (a) identification of the handwriting on the order for the rifle, its envelope and the accompanying money order as Oswald's; (b) the use in ordering the rifle of a false name corresponding to that on spurious identification documents found in Oswald's possession.

(5) *The shots could have been and probably were fired by Oswald.* This is demonstrated by (a) Oswald's admitted presence in the TSBD at the time of the assassination; (b) the presence on the southeast corner of the sixth floor of a homemade paper bag bearing Oswald's left index finger print and right palm print; (c) the presence on the rifle barrel of Oswald's palm print; (d) the presence in a crevice on the rifle of fibers taken from the shirt worn by Oswald at the time of his arrest; (e) the absence of any evidence pointing to the probability that any other person in the TSBD fired the shots.

That is the minimal case against Oswald. It will be noticed that in no detail does it require the acceptance of eyewitness testimony, disputed or undisputed. It is corroborated by the weight of the available eyewitness testimony, but for our purpose we need not even consider that. It is also corroborated by the physical evidence demonstrating that Patrolman Tippit was killed by bullets fired from a revolver found in Oswald's possession at the time of his arrest, but we need not consider that.

No one has yet suggested any basis for controverting any

part of what I have described as the minimal case. Of course, it does not conclusively establish that Oswald killed the President. It is in theory possible that some other person or persons either used Oswald's rifle to shoot the President or used his pistol to shoot Tippit, or both. But in the absence of evidence that it was physically impossible for Oswald to have done both killings, or of evidence pointing strongly to the probability that one killing, or both, were done by someone else, a jury might be expected to conclude on the basis of the minimal case alone that Oswald was the killer. No such discrediting evidence has been adduced, nor has its possible existence been made even remotely plausible.

The minimal case is supported rather than negated by what eyewitness testimony is available. But as every trial lawyer knows, eyewitness testimony is notoriously unreliable as compared with physical evidence. It is hardly cause for concern in any garden-variety criminal case that eyewitnesses disagree about such matters as how many shots were fired, whether a man was 5'11" or 5'8", was wearing a white or a light-colored jacket, had bushy hair or simply needed a haircut. Disagreements on matters of this kind are the everyday grist of the trial courts. The minimal case against Oswald is far stronger than that against many criminal defendants who are with perfect propriety convicted and sentenced every day. So far as eyewitness testimony goes, it needs to be remembered that in most criminal prosecutions there is either none at all or far less than was available here.

The discrepancies of evidence recorded by the commission are marginal. When there is a conflict of eyewitness testimony, someone has to be believed and someone disbelieved. Other indices of veracity aside, the basis on which choices of this kind are normally made is to ask oneself, consciously or unconsciously, which of the conflicting versions better accords with what is known to be true. There always comes a point in fact finding at which one says to himself: "This is the way it probably happened; now let us see how the hypothesis stands up." In that sense, any fact-finding process always involves at some stage the formation of a hypothesis. Here the evidence against which the hypothesis was tested was as the weight of the initial evidence compelled it to be, that Oswald acting alone was the killer. The question about the Warren Commission, as about any fact-finding body, is whether it made proper use of its working hypothesis. Did it close its mind to other possibilities? Did it refuse to deal with evidence inconsistent with its hypothesis? Did it suppress evidence? The answer to all these questions revealed by perusal of the report is an emphatic negative. Only someone irrevocably wedded to a contrary hypothesis could honestly (or would dishonestly) say that the Warren Commission was guilty of faults such as these.

One of the revisionists has said that when the full truth is known the Warren Commission report "will rank in history with the finding that Dreyfus was guilty of treason." The comparison is instructive, for it presents us with a measure of what would have had to be the case for the Warren Commission to suppress or ignore the truth about the President's assassination. The Dreyfus case involved a corrupt conspiracy among a reactionary group of French army officers to promote their own political ends by pinning the theft of certain secret documents on a Jewish army officer and, later, by suppressing evidence of his innocence. It would have required rottenness in an entire caste to achieve its purpose; in the end it failed because even in as monolithic a group as the French officer corps there was a Colonel Picquart who refused to be even a silent party to such degradation. The revisionists would have us believe that a similar conspiracy must have existed among the much more diverse group who made up the commission and its staff. It will take more than vague references to "the Establishment" to demonstrate the common bias of Earl Warren and Richard Russell, or the sinister motives that would unite John J. McCloy and Hale Boggs in a conspiracy to suppress the truth. And, of course, the issue extends beyond the seven members of the commission, on whom most of the fire has been concentrated. Any conspiracy to suppress evidence must also have included the staff, consisting mostly of outstanding young lawyers, several of them of distinctly liberal political persuasion, one of whom has had the compliment of being denounced on the floor of Congress as unfit to serve with the commission because of his membership in the Emergency Civil Liberties Committee and the American Civil Liberties Union. Only someone deeply ignorant of American society or deeply committed to a belief in its corruption, or both, could seriously maintain that a conspiracy of silence has been maintained by this group.

The commission's report convincingly demonstrates, as I have said, that Oswald, acting alone, was the assassin of the President. Let us now consider the significance of "acting alone." All that has been shown convincingly is that the immediate physical acts were those of Oswald alone. That has been demonstrated beyond reasonable doubt. The commission "found no evidence that anyone assisted Oswald in planning or carrying out the assassination." We may expect revisionist theories to move now from the discredited assertion that Oswald was not the killer or the sole killer to the much less disprovable assertion that he was the instrument of a conspiracy. We may also expect that the theories will all be variations on the theme that the conspiracy was composed of Texas oil millionaires or of Soviet (or perhaps Chinese or Cuban) agents, depending on the views of the proponent. It is necessary to admit that the commission did not succeed in excluding the possibility that Oswald was the instrument of either a rightist or a Communist conspiracy. Nor did it exclude the possibility that he was acting as the agent of Revilo P. Oliver or Mark Lane.[2] It is a little difficult to see how the commission, or any other human agency, could have done so. Even their careful review of what could be learned about Oswald's past could not fashion a net so fine that no significant event or acquaintance might slip through. Anyone who supposes

2. Oliver and Lane are prominent conspiracists.

that the commission could silence doubts of this order is deluded. We may confidently expect a spate of theories about Oswald's motivation. And it is not beyond the realm of possibility that one of them may turn out to have something to it. The commission's report did not purport to close what is obviously an unclosable door.

The revisionists have already fallen out among themselves. Mr. Leo Sauvage, who alone among them had the comparative good sense to ask questions rather than propound answers, has scornfully dismissed the third-rate James Bond thriller produced by Mr. Thomas Buchanan. We have yet to see whether Mr. Sauvage wishes to stand by his assertion that the case against Oswald is "a tissue of improbabilities, contradictions, and outright falsifications." The case of which he spoke was, of course, the case made to the press by the incredible antics of the Dallas authorities in the weekend of the assassination. That is not the case made by the Warren Commission. But the revisionists have already demonstrated that they intend to go on flogging a dead horse. Mr. Mark Lane, currently the most active of their number, has produced an appraisal that performs the interesting feat of attacking the report without once confronting its central findings. Instead, he devotes himself to the easy but now irrelevant task of attacking the inaccuracies in District Attorney Wade's oafish public statements. And Mr. Lane has the temerity to assert that he has the name of a witness to the Tippit shooting that the commission does not know about, without vouchsafing an explanation of his refusal to reveal the name when he testified before the commission.

What was merely tiresome in the days before the commission made its report is now mischievous. Mr. Lane and his friends are of course entitled to carry on. But they deserve attention if, and only if, they confront the central findings of the commission and demonstrate their falsity in any regard. These findings, to repeat, are: (1) *All the wounds sustained by President Kennedy and Governor Connally were inflicted by bullets fired from the rear and above.* (2) *All the shots were fired from the sixth-floor window of the Texas School Book Depository (TSBD).* (3) *The shots were fired from the Mannlicher-Carcano rifle found on the sixth floor of the TSBD.* (4) *Oswald was the owner of the rifle used in the assassination.* (5) *The shots could have been and probably were fired by Oswald.* None of these findings depends on resolving conflicts among eyewitnesses of the kind abundantly present in the perception of any disturbing event. This central core of physical evidence is the case against Lee Harvey Oswald. It is the case that would have had to be discredited in a court of law if Oswald had lived to be tried. It is the case that the revisionists must discredit if they wish us to believe that their a priori point of view of history happens this time to record a fact rather than an ideologue's fantasy.

An English Judge Praises *The Warren Commission Report*

Lord Devlin

The investigation into Kennedy's assassination drew the attention of legal experts from around the world. *The Warren Commission Report* was read avidly by them, as were other books and articles criticizing the commission's handling of the investigation and/or advancing conspiracy theories of their own. Not surprisingly, these experts were divided as to their opinions of the relative merits of the various interpretations, but a surprising number of them concurred with the commission's conclusions and praised the commission for doing a near-impossible job speedily and thoroughly.

Lord Devlin, an English judge, is perhaps typical of the foreign observers who applauded the commission for a job well done. At the time of Kennedy's death, Devlin was Lord of Appeals, a position roughly analogous to a U.S. federal circuit court judge. This article is an excerpt from an article he wrote for *Atlantic Monthly*, an American magazine, about *The Warren Commission Report*. In it he analyzes the facts of the assassination as well as the commission's handling of them.

As you read, consider the following questions:
1. What does Devlin regard as the major strength of *The Warren Commission Report*? Do you agree with his analysis? If so, why? If not, why not?

Lord Devlin, "Death of a President: The Established Facts," *Atlantic Monthly*, March 1965. Copyright © 1965 by the Literary Estate of Lord Devlin. Reproduced by permission.

2. What does Devlin regard as the major weakness of *The Warren Commission Report?* Do you agree with his analysis? If so, why? If not, why not?

The Lord Chief Justice of England is *ex officio* the chief coroner of the realm, an office he has held since time immemorial. There is therefore to an English mind something fitting in the idea that the inquiry into the death of President Kennedy, in its scope and importance the greatest inquest that has ever been held, should have been presided over by the Chief Justice of the United States. It is an inquest whose verdict was of universal concern; for John F. Kennedy was not only the President of the United States; he was also the captain of the free world. Consequently, the *Report of the Warren Commission* was clearly intended to be read and discussed in many countries outside the United States. I hope therefore that it will not be thought impertinent on my part if I attempt an appraisal of it.

It is a monumental work. Even after taking into account the quality and quantity of the staff which assisted the Commission and the resources which it had at its command, its production within ten months is an outstanding achievement. The mass of material is superbly organized. The structure is clear. Each fact is to be found in its proper place to sustain each conclusion. The minor conclusions support the major, and on the major the verdict rests. There is nothing anywhere to baffle or bemuse the critic. If he wants to dispute a conclusion, major or minor, he can find out with the greatest ease what sustains it and what it in turn sustains.

The first chapter of the report contains the summary and the twelve major conclusions. There are seven other chapters. The second and the fifth are mainly narrative, the second being the story of the death of President Kennedy and the fifth the story of the detention and death of Oswald, the man against whom the verdict is given. The eighth chapter deals with the arrangements for the protection of the President and falls outside the scope of this review. It is in the remaining four chapters that the conclusions which support the verdict are expressed and justified. . . .

My task is to consider the four chapters that sustain the verdict. The object of the inquiry was not to secure the posthumous conviction of Oswald. He is beyond human justice. If it had been certain that nothing could emerge from the inquiry except his guilt, there would have been no object in it. If that is all that does emerge from it, the episode is over and the book is closed. The object was to uncover the acts of the man or men who were privy to the murder. But the inquiry necessarily began with Oswald as the chief suspect, and its scope depended on whether the suspicion could be proved. If it could, the search could be limited to those among whom he moved and who could have acted through and with him. If it could not, the whole field was open and the inquiry began without a clue.

So the first question inevitably became whether Oswald was guilty, and that matter is dealt with in chapters III and IV. If he was, then the second question is whether anyone else was guilty. That matter is dealt with in chapters VI and VII. The Commission answers the first question affirmatively and the second negatively. The two answers need therefore to be reviewed quite differently. In relation to the first, what has to be considered is whether the evidence assembled by the Commission proves sufficiently the guilt of Oswald. In relation to the second, what has to be considered is whether the inquiry was sufficiently wide and searching to bring all the relevant facts to light, for on the facts that the Commission brought to light there is no evidence of any accomplice. . . .

In reviewing the conclusions reached about Oswald's guilt in chapters III and IV, I shall, as a reader would do in his own mind, pick out the factors that seem to me to be of the greatest significance.

There was one eyewitness, and one only, of the deed who claimed to identify Oswald as the perpetrator. Howard L. Brennan was watching the parade from a point directly opposite the Texas School Book Depository. Less than a minute after the President's car had passed that point Brennan saw a man, whom he later identified as Oswald, fire a rifle from the southeast-corner window on the sixth floor of the depository. This makes a natural foundation for the case against Oswald. But the Commission—rightly, I think—does not treat it as such. Brennan was 120 feet from the window. He gave a good description of the man he saw, but he was not clearly and consistently sure of his ability to make a positive identification. Moreover, the identification lineup took place after Brennan had seen Oswald's picture on television. The Commission therefore does not base its conclusion concerning the identity of the assassin on Brennan's identification. It does not go further than to say that the man in the window seen by Brennan closely resembled Oswald.

This the inquiry into the assassination divides itself into two parts. Was the President killed by shots fired from the depository window? This is the subject matter of Chapter III. If so, was it Oswald who fired them? This is the subject matter of Chapter IV. Thirty-two minutes after the assassination, police officers searching the depository found three empty cartridge cases on the floor near the window which Brennan had identified. Ten minutes later in the opposite corner of the room they found a Mannlicher-Carcano rifle fitted with a telescopic sight. Experts testified that the three used cartridge cases had been fired from the rifle; and further, that two bullets (one in fragments found in the front seat of the presidential car, and the other on the stretcher in which Governor Connally was carried into the hospital) were also fired from the same rifle.

There were several eyewitnesses besides Brennan who saw a rifle being fired from the window. The three important ones are those who acted on what they saw before there was any time for retrospective imagination to get to work. There was Brennan himself, who immediately reported what he had seen to a police officer. His description of the gunman was most probably the basis of the description that was circulated by the police fifteen minutes after the murder. The second was a witness who also immediately reported to a police officer, who transmitted the evidence to headquarters six minutes after the murder. The third was a photographer in a press car in the motorcade, who called out to the others in the car with him and took a photograph of the window.

All this is simple to follow and appears to me to establish quite conclusively that the shots that killed the President were fired from the depository. The rest of the evidence is corroborative. There is medical evidence about the nature of the wounds to show that the bullets were fired from above and behind and also evidence that a bullet fragment struck the windshield of the car from behind.

The Commission examined and dismissed the suggestion that shots were fired from in front—that is, from the triple underpass which at the time of the murder the President's car was approaching. It is obviously convenient to deal with this suggestion in this chapter, but it is not strictly relevant to the question of Oswald's guilt. If shots had been fired from another place, the fact would show only that some other person, presumably an associate of Oswald, was also taking part in the crime.

I now turn to the subject matter of Chapter IV—that is, the evidence to prove that Oswald was the man who fired the shots. Apart from the identification by Brennan, it is all indirect and can be divided into four categories. First, there is the evidence which connects Oswald with the actual shooting. Second, there is evidence that three quarters of an hour after the murder, he shot Patrolman Tippit so as avoid a possible arrest. Third, there is evidence that he attempted to hide in a cinema and that when he was actually arrested half an hour after Tippit's murder, he resisted with violence. Finally, there is evidence that in April, 1963, Oswald had attempted to shoot Major General Edwin A. Walker, whom the report describes as "an active and controversial figure on the American political Scene." This is the least important category, and it can be mentioned briefly. The charge is based on Oswald's admission to his wife, corroborated by a note which he left for her before the attempt and in which he refers to the contingency of his being taken prisoner, and by the fact that there were found among his possessions three photographs of General Walker's house taken by a camera which he owned.

The chief evidence to connect Oswald with the shooting of the President is as follows. In March, 1963, Oswald bought under an assumed name the Mannlicher-Carcano rifle found in the depository. In November, 1963, Oswald and his family were living at Irving, about fifteen miles from Dallas. Oswald lived there only on weekends, and he traveled in and out of Dallas in a car driven by a neighbor, Mr. Frazier, who also worked at the depository. On the morning of November 21, which was a Thursday, Oswald asked Frazier to drive him home that evening so that he could get some curtain rods. On the following morning, the day of the assassination, Frazier drove Oswald back to the depository. Oswald had with him a large brown paper bag, which he said contained curtain rods. A brown paper bag of a size and shape that might have contained either the disassembled rifle or curtain rods was found alongside the window from which the shot was fired with a palm print of Oswald's on it. Oswald remained in the building during the lunch hour and might have been on the sixth floor at the time of the shooting. The ownership of a rifle used in a murder does not prove that the owner was the murderer, but it calls for an explanation. Likewise, a story about curtain rods can do with some amplification. So it is important to see what was said on these points by Oswald during his interrogation. "Interrogation" is rather a grand word to use, for he was questioned by the Texas police in a very haphazard way. No contemporary record was kept, and the evidence of it consists of memoranda prepared afterward by police officers who from time to time took part in it. It would be unsafe to rely on anything which depended for its force on the actual words used, but the record can be relied on, generally, for the topics discussed and the way in which they were handled by Oswald. He offered no explanation. He simply denied that he had ever bought a rifle or that he had ever said anything to Frazier about curtain rods. The Commission was entitled to ask itself why he lied.

No fiction writer would provide for the assassination of a public figure in circumstances such as these without assuring his readers that the assassin was a marksman of the

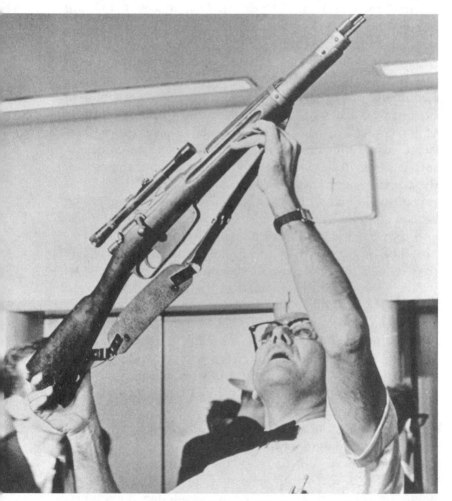

A Dallas police officer examines the rifle that was used to kill President Kennedy. The rifle was found in the Texas School Book Depository Building.

highest order. It may therefore come as a surprise to members of the public to be told by the experts that the target was an easy one and well within the capabilities of Oswald, who had been trained as a marksman in the Marine Corps. In the Marine Corps he was said to be a good shot, slightly above average, and by comparison with the ordinary civilian, an excellent shot. This, of course, is not positive evidence against Oswald. It only goes to rebut the suggestion that he could not have killed the President because it was beyond his capabilities to do so. In any event, the point goes to the existence of a conspiracy rather than to the guilt of Oswald. It would not meet the evidence of complicity; it would suggest no more than that Oswald was the accomplice of a superior marksman. The evidence connecting Oswald with the assassination of the President would in my opinion be insufficient if there were not evidence connecting him with the murder of Patrolman Tippit. It is most unlikely that Oswald would have murdered Tippit if he had not previously been concerned in the killing of the President. The two things hang together.

Two witnesses who saw the shooting of Tippit and seven who saw the flight of the murderer with revolver in hand identified Oswald as the man. None of them had much more than a glimpse of him. I have what may be an unreasonable distrust of evidence of identification in sensational cases under such conditions. In considering the evidence of persons who claimed to have seen Ruby and Oswald together, the Commission recorded that it had "encountered numerous clear mistakes of identification." Mistaken identification has probably accounted for more miscarriages of justice than any other single factor. Several of the witnesses had seen Oswald's picture in the newspaper or on television before the lineup. I am left with the impression that the value of this testimony might at a trial have been much reduced by defense counsel. Nevertheless, nine is a considerable number. The value of their testimony must depend to a great extent on the impression of reliability which they gave, and only the Commission can evaluate that. For those who neither saw nor heard the witnesses there is more impressive testimony. First, the man who was undoubtedly the murderer was seen immediately after to eject cartridge cases from his revolver. Four of these were picked up by three independent witnesses and given to the police. They were fired from a revolver which had been purchased by Oswald and which was found in his possession at the time of his arrest within half an hour of the murder of Tippit. Second, in the hot pursuit of the murderer after the crime, he was last seen in a parking lot behind a gasoline service station. Within ten minutes of Tippit's murder, Oswald's jacket was found under one of the cars in the parking lot.

Ten minutes later a man without a jacket ducked into a shop as a police car was passing and so attracted the attention of a Mr. Brewer, the manager of the store. Brewer followed him and saw him go into a theater a few doors away without buying a ticket. The police were sent for, the lights in the theater were turned up, and Brewer pointed out the man he had seen. A police officer approached him and told him to stand up. The man did so; then he struck at the officer and drew a gun. This man, whom the police arrested, was Oswald. The explanation he gave for his being in the movie at this time in the afternoon was that there would be no more work in the depository that day owing to the confusion in the building.

If the case against Oswald is stripped of everything that does not amount to practical certainty, what is left is this. He was in the building at the time of the assassination of the President and could have been on the sixth floor. The President was killed by a gun which belonged to Oswald and which he falsely denied buying or owning. The man who fired it was not unlike Oswald. Three quarters of an hour later Patrolman Tippit was shot with a revolver belonging to Oswald. Oswald's jacket was found along the path taken by the murderer in flight. Then Oswald was found with the revolver in his possession, and he used violence in resisting arrest. He was a man who had attempted assassination before. In the report these bare bones are fully fleshed. An exhaustive investigation has produced a mass of corroborative evidence and nothing at all to shake the natural conclusion. . . .

So it seems to me to be quite unreasonable to suggest that the Commission, when it embarked upon the second part of its task, should have looked for a conspiracy to which Oswald was not a party. There are three factors on the surface of events which at the beginning must have made it look more likely than not that Oswald had accomplices. I have not in mind as one of them the rumored shots from the triple underpass. It is highly unlikely that two sets of conspirators would have arranged a time in advance irrespective of the point on the route, or that they could have arranged a point on the route which would have suited both equally.

The first superficial factor is the doubt whether a crime of this magnitude and difficulty can be successfully committed by a man who is acting entirely alone. If Oswald was acting alone, luck was with him all the way.

The second factor is the killing of Oswald by Ruby, which by a curious coincidence gives rise to an improbability of the same sort. To British eyes at first—though the view has been changed by the Commission's descriptions of activities at the Dallas police headquarters—to kill a man while in the custody of the police at their headquarters would be a far more difficult task than to kill a statesmen in a public parade. Was this task also accomplished by a man acting alone and with nothing to prompt him except his own inspiration? The coincidence remains even after all the facts are told. Oswald and Ruby both emerge as curious characters acting with motives that seem incomprehensible to the ordinary man. It is not surprising that, as the Commission says, "almost immediately speculation arose that Ruby had acted on behalf of members of a conspiracy who had planned the killing of President Kennedy and wanted to silence Oswald."

The third factor is Oswald's Communist background. In

1959 he went to Moscow and applied for Soviet citizenship. He married a Russian girl and remained in Russia until June, 1962. His Marxist sympathies remained with him. Back in the United States he kept in touch with the Soviet Embassy and engaged in Fair Play for Cuba activities. Less than two months before the assassination he had gone to Mexico City, where he visited the Cuban and Russian Embassies.

This third factor, while it lends force to the idea of a conspiracy, has also the effect of limiting the area of search. Unless something appears to show that Oswald's Communist sympathies were not genuine, there is no need to look except in a precautionary way for other sources for the conspiracy.

There is another limiting factor in the time. Oswald's employment in the depository began on October 15. No detailed plotting for the assassination could begin until the motorcade route was known. The planning of the route was not started until November 4 and not finally announced until November 19. But the destination, the trade market in Dallas, was announced on November 15, and after that date there was at any rate a probability that the motorcade would pass the depository. This leaves a bare week for a plot to be made. The movements of Oswald and of Ruby during that period would obviously have to be closely investigated. The other period for close investigation of the movements of Ruby would be the period between the death of the President and the death of Oswald. If Oswald's death was planned by others besides Ruby, it must have been during that period that the plan was made.

The second period is dealt with in great detail in the report. Ruby's movements are accounted for almost hour by hour. The first period is not. All that the report says of Ruby's movements during that period is that he gave several detailed accounts of them and that scrutiny "has revealed no indication of any unusual activity." Oswald's activities over the same period are not the subject of any specific finding, the days are not dealt with chronologically, and I have not found any indication that they were closely investigated. This is rather surprising in a report that is so careful of detail. Of course, Oswald lived alone in Dallas, and unlike Ruby, had not the contacts which would make his normal activities easily discoverable. We know that at his wife's suggestion he did not go home to Irving for the weekend of November 16 and 17. We are not told whether in the week that followed he was at work during the normal hours.

Apart from this, all the lines of inquiry that one can think of are pursued in the report. Oswald's finances are inspected. All his known associations after his return to the States are probed. His activities on his visit to Mexico City have of course been examined in detail. Any evidence that might suggest the presence of another man at the window at the time of the shooting has been carefully considered.

All this is negative. On the positive side the careers of Oswald and Ruby have been traced from birth. An appendix is devoted to each of them. The picture that emerges of them both makes it, to my mind, more likely that each of them would have acted as a solitary than as a conspirator. Their motives are inexplicable by ordinary standards, but there is something in the character of each that makes them at least plausible. It is impossible within a reasonable compass to give the effect of all this evidence, whether it be positive or negative. I can only say that after reading it all and apart from the one omission I have noted (which by itself affords too slender a basis for criticism, for there may well be some explanation I have overlooked), I am left with the impression of a searching and objective investigation and a completely impartial analysis. The appropriate conclusion cannot be put better than the Commission puts it.

> Because of the difficulty of proving negatives to a certainty the possibility of others being involved with either Oswald or Ruby cannot be established categorically, but if there is any such evidence it has been beyond the reach of the United States and has not come to the attention of this Commission.

A History Professor Praises *The Warren Commission Report*

Jacob Cohen

Perhaps the main problem facing the Warren Commission was that it had to present one, and only one, version of how President Kennedy was murdered. The commission did not enjoy the luxury of being able to present the facts without also offering a framework within which to interpret those facts. Consequently, it had to arrive at a decision as to which scenario made the most sense, even though some of the facts of the case did not always support that one scenario. Meanwhile, its critics, who were not so hampered, were left free to criticize the various inconsistencies and oddities in *The Warren Commission Report* without having to present a coherent counterversion of how the president was killed.

Jacob Cohen taught history at Yale and Brandeis Universities before becoming a full-time author. His works include *Honest Verdict* (1967), the first book-length defense of *The Warren Commission Report*. In this article, an excerpt from an article he wrote for *Frontier* magazine, he outlines what conspiracists must prove in order to disprove the commission's finding that Oswald acted alone.

As you read, consider the following questions:
1. Why does Cohen defend *The Warren Commission Report*? Does his reasoning make sense to you? If so, why? If not, why not?

2. If you were Mark Lane or some other conspiracist, how would you respond to Cohen's argument? Does this argument make more sense than Cohen's? If so, why? If not, why not?

Anyone who has read the principal critics of the Warren Commission Report and tried to piece together what *they* think happened on Dealey Plaza, about 12:30 P.M. the day of the assassination, may have shared with me the need to reassert his grip on the world. It was the Warren Commission's job to tell the world what single set of events occurred in Dallas. As the Commission formed an idea of what happened, what plausibly could have happened, given the constellation of incontrovertible evidence, the Commission discounted apparent contradictions in the evidence which pointed in impossible or utterly unlikely directions. There is nothing sinister in this. Quite obviously the Commission could not have submitted a report which said in effect:

> This is a fascinating subject full of awesome contradictions. We are of several minds on the number of assassins. There may have been one or there may have been four. Since we can't make up our minds, we thought we would just present the evidence in all its complexity and let the world decide for itself.

I believe it was the Commission's commitment to the singular actuality of the event which many critics have mistaken for an inflexible and closed-minded commitment to the theory of one assassin.

The critics, on the other hand, have been playing by different rules. Pursuing a strategy of pure attack, they have displayed a capacity to live with contradictions which would be the envy of any Zen Buddhist. They do not join the Commission in asking: What happened? Their controlling question seems to be: What's wrong with the Warren Report?—a method which has led them to some inspired kibitzing and implied accusations which are sinister beyond belief. . . .

The Wounds

According to the Warren Commission, all of [the] wounds, Kennedy's and Connally's, were inflicted by two bullets. The first shot hit the President very high in the back at a point described by an eyewitness to the autopsy, Secret Service man Roy H. Kellerman, as "on the shoulder . . . in the large muscle behind shoulder and the neck, just below it. . . ." The autopsy itself places this wound at a point "14 centimeters from the tip of the right acromion process [near the tip of the shoulder] and 14 centimeters [5½ inches] below the tip of the right mastoid process [which is behind the ear].". . . Actually, we would have to know the length of Kennedy's neck to have a precise idea of where the autopsy measurements leave us. Now, according to the Commission, the bullet which caused this wound came from above and behind the President; it passed through his neck leaving internal damage which is described in considerable detail in the autopsy, then hit Connally, who was in a jumpseat in front of the President, causing the injuries to Connally's back, rib, chest, wrist, and thigh. This is the famous "double hit," one bullet striking both Kennedy and Connally, causing all of Connally's wounds; and all critics and most of the defenders of the Warren Report, including the present one, agree that the double hit is indispensable to the Commission's theory of a single assassin. As for the massive wound in Kennedy's skull, according to the Commission, it was caused by a second bullet which struck the President at the base of the skull, leaving a small wound of entry, and then blasted out the side of his head. The Commission claims that parts of only two bullets were recovered: one almost perfectly intact (Exhibit 399) was found in the Parkland Hospital in Dallas where Kennedy and Connally were treated immediately after the shooting. That bullet, says the Report, perpetrated the double hit. Additionally, fairly large fragments of a second bullet were found in the Presidential limousine. Ballistics tests performed in the FBI laboratories in Washington the day after the assassination showed that both bullets had been fired from the rifle (Oswald's) recovered from the sixth floor of the Texas School Book Depository. Two shots, then, two bullets, from the same source, caused all the damage. A third shot missed, and so is the bullet missing, according to the Warren Commission.

The critics have disputed this version of the assassination in several ways. First, they challenge the Commission's (and the autopsy's) claim that the throat wound was a wound of exit, claiming it was a wound of entrance caused by an assassin situated in front of the President; they deny, therefore, that the bullet, which indubitably struck Kennedy somewhere in the back, went on to exit from his throat and hit Connally. Accordingly, the critics must believe that this bullet lodged in Kennedy at least temporarily, and some critics have suggested that the nearly whole bullet recovered at the Parkland Hospital (Exhibit 399) was dislodged from Kennedy's back. Second, the critics claim that the actual wound in Kennedy's back was lower than is indicated in the autopsy, a point related to the first one, since a bullet which hit Kennedy lower on the back could not have exited from his throat at the required downward angle. Third, the critics, at least most of them, contend that the massive wound on the right side of Kennedy's head was an entry wound inflicted by an assassin somewhere to the right of the President; they therefore dispute the autopsy's contention that there was a small wound of entry in the base of Kennedy's skull and that the large default in the right side of Kennedy's head was a wound of exit. Since the location of a wound in a man's back and the question of whether or not he has a small hole in the base of his skull are matters of the simplest fact, it follows that the critics who dispute the autopsy findings are claiming that the autopsy surgeons deliberately falsified their findings and, since the autopsy examination at the Naval Medical Center in Bethesda, Md., took place the night of the assassination, that this deception began the very night of the assassination. Fourth, the critics argue that the Parkland Hospital bullet (Exhibit 399) is too heavy and unmutilated to have done the damage attributed to it by the double-hit theory. . . .

But the critics never measure the angles required by their own criticism, or pursue leads into reality, at least not in print. Having raised the specter of a frontal hit, no critic has yet checked out the plausibility of such a hit. We hear about shots that came from the "grassy knoll" but are not told that the knoll is some 200 feet long and that eyewitnesses place the source of those shots from one end to the other; in other words, the "grassy knoll" is not one place, but many. A wooden fence ran across the top of the knoll and an assassin would have to have been behind that fence in order not to have been seen by at least one of the some 260 known eyewitnesses to the shooting. And from most of the points behind the fence on top of the knoll the President's car would have been obscured by the trees, bushes, cement structures and by persons we know to have been standing in the way. That is why the only likely point for an assassin to have hit the President in the throat would have placed the killer considerably to the right of the President. . . . And such a shot, if it occurred, would have come from a point about thirty feet from and directly behind several people who were standing on the grassy knoll. Photographs of these onlookers, taken about three seconds after Kennedy's throat was creased, show them looking straight ahead and not back toward an explosion.

Critics' Theories Lack Substance

My point is that the critics never seem to check out their own hypotheses. Mark Lane announces that he has been to Dallas six times; that he has photographed the assassination scene from a helicopter; and has reinterviewed, for a movie he made, the witnesses who remember seeing smoke on the grassy knoll just after the shooting. (Not a single witness claims to have seen a gun, or a gunman, other than in the Book Depository Building.) Considering his interest in the assassination site, one would think that at some point Mr. Lane would have taken his camera to the spot where the smoke was reportedly seen and have checked out the location as a possible perch for the assassin. But, of course, Mr. Lane would then have to say in some systematic manner what *he* thinks happened in Dallas, and this he seems disinclined to do. . . .

Assuming there really was a shot from the knoll, the critics must believe that shots came from at least two very different directions (actually four as I shall demonstrate). For it is almost certain that at least one or two shots came from the Book Depository: Two eyewitnesses actually saw shots being fired from a rifle in the window of the sixth floor of the Depository and said as much to police immediately thereafter; three persons saw a gun in the window and exclaimed so to companions who recall their exclamations; a rifle and three shells were found on the same sixth floor and ballistics tests performed the next day in Washington showed that this rifle had fired a bullet which was found near Governor Connally's stretcher at the Parkland Hospital and the two large fragments of a bullet found in the Presidential limousine; three men on the fifth floor, just under the murder window, heard what may have been the shells hitting the floor, and report other impressions which confirm the presence of an assassin above them; at least one of Kennedy's wounds, and Connally's, were inflicted from a shot above and behind; and many earwitnesses thought shots came from the Book Depository. So it is not exactly controversial to suggest that at least one gunman was up there firing away. If we suppose, then, that shots came from at least two directions, the question arises as to how many earwitnesses heard shots coming from both the grassy knoll and the Book Depository. In other words, how many people heard the event, as it must have occurred, if the critics are correct? And the answer is: not one. But many eye- and earwitnesses, not quite a majority, heard and saw the assassination essentially as the Commission reconstructed it, in terms of the source and number of shots, and almost every witness indicated that he thought the shots came from *one* direction. Earwitness testimony, of course, is notoriously muddled; contradictions cling to the remains of every human event. But if one were to take the Commission's version of what happened and then force the critics to say what *they* think happened, placing the two versions side by side, one would conclude, I believe, that the Commission had somewhat the better of it on the score of eyewitness testimony.

Nor can the critics stop at two assassins. Recall that both critics and defenders of the Warren Report agree that the President was hit in the back from the back, that he had a wound in his throat, and on the right side of his head, and that Governor Connally was also struck by a shot fired from behind him. Analysis of the Zapruder films further shows that Governor Connally could not have been hit from the Book Depository after frame 235 of the Zapruder films because at that point he turned out of range. Students of the assassination will here recall that the critics have proved conclusively that one assassin could not have hit Connally and Kennedy separately because one rifleman would not have had time to refire before Connally turned away. Were we to feed all this data into a fairly simple computer, a card would come out entitled "Number of Assassins," saying: One assassin in front of President causing throat wound; second assassin behind President administering back wound; third assassin behind Governor Connally probably causing all of his wounds with one shot; and (if one believes that the massive wound in Kennedy's skull was administered from the right as all the leading critics except Edward Epstein contend) a fourth assassin to the right. Of Edward Epstein's implied theory that there were only two assassins, both in the Book Depository, one shooting Connally in the back and head, we must conclude that it is impossible because it cannot explain how Kennedy could have been wounded in the throat four seconds before he was struck in the head. The critic who has written most forthrightly on the assassination, Vincent Salandria, now believes that Governor Connally was not hit until Zapruder frame 292, by which time the Governor had turned sharply to his right, virtually facing the grassy knoll, so that his back was exposed only to the south side of Dealey Plaza. If things happened that way, we now have a fourth assassin at a point diametrically opposite the knoll and about a block away from the Book Depository. If Salandria is right concerning what is required of an alternative theory of the assassination, and I think he is, four widely separated assassins fired five times almost simultaneously: Kennedy back; Kennedy head; Connally back; Kennedy throat; and the shot that, all agree, missed. And, if Connally was struck more than once, there were six shots or more. That is a lot of missing bullets. And remember, none of these assassins was seen coming, going, or killing. Small wonder that the critics, except Salandria, have little inclination to pursue their own theories to their logical conclusions.

But what of the doctors at Parkland who said that the wound in Kennedy's throat looked like an entrance wound? And at this point one must say, as the Warren Commission said, that they were simply mistaken. It looked to them like an entry wound, but it wasn't. And the mistake is certainly easy to understand to anyone who accepts the possibility of human error. We know that the people at Parkland had only a moment with the neck wound before it was widened to perform a tracheotomy and that the doctors at Dallas never even turned the President over, and therefore did not know about the wound in his back. In speculating on the source of a wound simply by its external appearance they broke a cardinal rule of their craft, for the forensic pathologist's essential technique is to interpret wounds according to the whole configuration of damage. "Amateurish" is the way one world-renowned forensic pathologist described to me the performance of doctors who would speculate on the source of a wound without relating the wound to the accompanying data. And by the time the doctors testified before the Commission, in March, 1964, they were saying as much about themselves:

Mr. Arlen Specter [Commission counsel]. Based on your observations on the neck wound alone did you have a sufficient basis to form an opinion as to whether it was an entrance or an exit wound?

Dr. Charles J. Carrico. No, sir; we did not. Not having completely evaluated all the wounds, traced out the course of the bullets, this wound would have been compatible with either entrance or exit wound depending on the size, the velocity, the tissue structure and so forth.

Other doctors testifying before the Commission repeated that the wound had looked much like an entrance wound, but all agreed that they had not had enough information to judge and that the presence of a back wound, and damage in the neck, in perfect alignment, was conclusive. In the passion of those dreadful days many people rushed to offer their expertise to posterity; it was a problem that continually plagued a Commission which did not have the leisure to play with contradictions as the critics do, and had to go about the business of discarding mistakes.

Therefore, to support the Commission on the question of the throat wound one need only believe that some doctors in Dallas misinterpreted the nature of a wound they saw fleetingly. Since the doctors themselves freely admitted their error before the Commission, it does not seem extreme to take them at their considered word. On the other hand, if one is to support the critics on the question of the throat wound, one must be prepared to accept the notion of massive duplicity: an autopsy examination rigged from the first moment; a deliberately inaccurate autopsy report; lying testimony on the part of the autopsy doctors (the interested reader is directed to Volume II of Warren Commission testimony where the doctors testify in great detail concerning their medical findings). Understand that if the critics are correct, these doctors are fabricating nearly everything they say. If the doctors were deceiving all and sundry the night of the assassination, then they must have been ordered to do so that day or before. By whom? Why? Merely to frame one and only one man? Let some critic deny that these questions are inescapably implied in his analysis.

Nor can the critics simply concede the argument over the throat wound and go on to other encounters. If, in fact, the throat wound was *not* a wound of entry, then the supposition is strongly enforced that it was the wound of exit the Commission said it was; and if a bullet did exit from the throat in the way described by the Commission, then it could not easily have missed the Governor, who was seated directly in front of Kennedy. And if the Governor was indeed hit by that bullet, the double hit is confirmed. With each concession from the critics, the Commission's case is reconstituted. Such is the interlocking character of reality.

4

NEGATIVE RESPONSES TO THE WARREN COMMISSION REPORT

CHAPTER PREFACE

While legal experts were praising *The Warren Commission Report*, other interested observers were belittling it. Many of these observers, known as conspiracists, believed that a conspiracy was responsible for Kennedy's assassination, and they criticized the fact that the commission seemed to arrive at its conclusions without seriously considering any other possibility than that Oswald had acted alone. They pointed to a number of coincidences and hard-to-explain facts as evidence of the existence of a conspiracy. They were also critical of the fact that the Warren Commission did not have any investigators of its own to track down leads or to locate and examine crucial documents. Instead, it was forced to rely upon the FBI and the CIA to perform these types of investigative services. Many conspiracists believed that these two agencies were somehow involved in the assassination.

In time, other government bodies besides the Warren Commission would conduct their own investigations into Kennedy's death. A Louisiana district attorney, Jim Garrison, claimed to have discovered the existence of a plot that was hatched in and around New Orleans. Although he was never able to convict any one individual of conspiracy, he convinced two juries that a conspiracy to kill Kennedy had existed.

During the mid-1970s, both houses of the U.S. Congress established select committees to look into the circumstances surrounding Kennedy's murder. The House concluded that a conspiracy led by organized crime had killed the president. The Senate rejected the idea that Kennedy had died at the hands of conspirators, but it did disclose that the FBI and CIA had not told the Warren Commission everything they knew about either Lee Harvey Oswald or Jack Ruby. The Senate committee was particularly concerned to discover that, at the time of Kennedy's assassination, the CIA was actively plotting to assassinate Fidel Castro, whom many believed to be the mastermind behind Kennedy's death.

In 1992 Congress established the Assassination Records Review Board (ARRB) as a way to locate, examine, and release to the public government records pertaining to the assassination. In the process of doing its work, the ARRB discovered that Kennedy's autopsy was surrounded by a number of discrepancies and irregularities. This revelation gave rise to further speculation that the federal government was involved in covering up the facts relating to Kennedy's death.

Jim Garrison Believes in a Government Conspiracy

Jim Garrison and Playboy

Jim Garrison was the district attorney for New Orleans. In November 1966, he began having doubts about the Warren Commission's conclusion that Oswald had acted alone, and he started an informal investigation into the Kennedy assassination. In the process, he learned about a CIA facility just outside New Orleans where anti-Castro terrorists had been trained. Further investigation led Garrison to conclude that Kennedy had been killed by rogue agents of the CIA who had been trained at the New Orleans facility, and he began formal proceedings to bring them to trial. The investigation led to the 1967 arrest of Clay Shaw, a CIA operative. Shaw was indicted by a panel of three judges and tried in 1969. After a trial of thirty-nine days, Shaw was acquitted; the jury decided that Garrison had proved the existence of a conspiracy to kill Kennedy but not that Shaw was part of it.

In 1967 Garrison agreed to be interviewed by *Playboy* magazine. This article is an excerpt from that interview.

As you read, consider the following questions:
1. Does Garrison's argument as outlined in this article make sense? If so, why? If not, why not?
2. How might Garrison have responded to the suggestion that Fidel Castro was responsible for Kennedy's death?

PLAYBOY: According to your own former chief investigator, William Gurvich, the truth about the assassination has already been published in the Warren Report. After leaving your staff last June, he announced, "If there is any truth to any of Garrison's charges about there being a conspiracy, I haven't been able to find it." When members of your own staff have no faith in your case, how do you expect the public to be impressed?

GARRISON: First of all, I won't deny for a minute that for at least three months I trusted Bill Gurvich implicitly. He was never my "chief investigator"—that's his own terminology—because there was no such position on my staff while he worked for me. But two days before Christmas 1966, Gurvich, who operates a private detective agency, visited my office and told me he'd heard of my investigation and thought I was doing a wonderful job. He presented me with a beautiful color-TV set and asked if he could be of use in any capacity.

Well, right then and there, I should have sat back and asked myself a few searching questions—like how he had heard of my probe in the first place, since only the people we were questioning and a few of my staff, as far as I knew, were aware of what was going on at that time. We had been under way for only five weeks, remember. And I should also have recalled the old adage about Greeks bearing gifts. But I was desperately understaffed—I had only six aides available to work on the assassination inquiry full time—and here comes a trained private investigator offering his services free of charge. It was like a gift from the gods.

So I set Gurvich to work; and for the next couple of months, he did an adequate job of talking to witnesses, taking photographs, etc. But then, around March, I learned that he had been seeing Walter Sheridan of NBC.[1] Well, this didn't bother me at first, because I didn't know then the role Sheridan was playing in this whole affair. But after word got back to me from my witnesses about Sheridan's threats and harassment, I began keeping a closer eye on Bill. I still didn't really think he was any kind of a double

---

1. Walter Sheridan was the special investigator for an NBC television special that portrayed Garrison in a very unfavorable light.

agent, but I couldn't help wondering why he was rubbing elbows with people like that.

Now, don't forget that Gurvich claims he became totally disgusted with our investigation at the time of Clay Shaw's arrest—yet for several months afterward he continued to wax enthusiastic about every aspect of our case, and I have a dozen witnesses who will testify to that effect. I guess this was something that should have tipped me off about Bill: He was always enthusiastic, never doubtful or cautionary, even when I or one of my staff threw out a hypothesis that on reflection we realized was wrong. And I began to notice how he would pick my mind for every scrap of fact pertaining to the case. So I grew suspicious and took him off the sensitive areas of the investigation and relegated him to chauffeuring and routine clerical duties.

This seemed to really bother him, and every day he would come into my office and pump me for information, complaining that he wasn't being told enough about the case. I still had nothing concrete against him and I didn't want to be unjust, but I guess my manner must have cooled perceptibly, because one day about two months before he surfaced in Washington, Bill just vanished from our sight. And with him, I'm sorry to confess, vanished a copy of our master file.

Gurvich Was a Spy

How do you explain such behavior? It's possible that Bill joined us initially for reasons of opportunism, seeing a chance to get in at the beginning of an earth-shaking case, and subsequently chickened out when he saw the implacable determination of some powerful agencies to destroy our investigation and discredit everyone associated with it. But I really don't believe Bill is that much of a coward. It's also possible that those who want to prevent an investigation learned early what we were doing and made a decision to plant somebody on the inside of the investigation. Let me stress that I have no secret documents or monitored telephone calls to support this hypothesis; it just seems to me the most logical explanation for Bill's behavior. Let me put it this way: If you were in charge of the CIA and willing to spend scores of millions of dollars on such relatively penny-ante projects as infiltrating the National Students Association, wouldn't you make an effort to infiltrate an investigation that could seriously damage the prestige of your agency?

PLAYBOY: How could your probe damage the prestige of the CIA and cause them to take countermeasures against you?

GARRISON: For the simple reason that a number of the men who killed the President were former employees of the CIA involved in its anti-Castro underground activities in and around New Orleans. The CIA knows their identity. So do I—and our investigation has established this without the shadow of a doubt. Let me stress one thing, however: We have no evidence that any official of the CIA was involved with the conspiracy that led to the President's death.

PLAYBOY: Do you lend no credence, then, to the charges of a former CIA agent, J. Garrett Underhill, that there was a conspiracy within the CIA to assassinate Kennedy?

GARRISON: I've become familiar with the case of Gary Underhill, and I've been able to ascertain that he was not the type of man to make wild or unsubstantiated charges. Underhill was an intelligence agent in World War Two and an expert on military affairs whom the Pentagon considered one of the country's top authorities on limited warfare. He was on good personal terms with the top brass in the Defense Department and the ranking officials in the CIA. He wasn't a full-time CIA agent, but he occasionally performed "special assignments" for the Agency. Several days after the President's assassination, Underhill appeared at the home of friends in New Jersey, apparently badly shaken, and charged that Kennedy was killed by a small group within the CIA. He told friends he believed his own life was in danger. We can't learn any more from Underhill, I'm afraid, because shortly afterward, he was found shot to death in his Washington apartment. The coroner ruled suicide, but he had been shot behind the left ear and the pistol was found under his left side—and Underhill was right-handed.

PLAYBOY: Do you believe Underhill was murdered to silence him?

GARRISON: I don't believe it and I don't disbelieve it. All I know is that witnesses with vital evidence in this case are certainly bad insurance risks. In the absence of further and much more conclusive evidence to the contrary, however, we must assume that the plotters were acting on their own rather than on CIA orders when they killed the President. As far as we have been able to determine, they were not in the pay of the CIA at the time of the assassination—and this is one of the reasons the President was murdered: I'll explain later what I mean by that. But the CIA could not face up to the American people and admit that its former employees had conspired to assassinate the President; so from the moment Kennedy's heart stopped beating, the Agency attempted to sweep the whole conspiracy under the rug. The CIA has spared neither time nor the taxpayers' money in its efforts to hide the truth about the assassination from the American people. In this respect, it has become an accessory after the fact in the assassination.

PLAYBOY: Do you have any conclusive evidence to support these accusations?

The CIA Hired Lawyers

GARRISON: . . . let's start with the fact that most of the attorneys for the hostile witnesses and defendants were hired by the CIA—through one or another of its covers. For example, a New Orleans lawyer representing Alvin Beauboeuf,[2] who has charged me with every kind of unethical practice except child molesting—I expect that allegation to come shortly before Shaw's trial—flew with Beauboeuf to Washington immediately after my office subpoenaed him,

---

2. Alvin Beauboeuf was a friend of David Ferrie, whom Garrison believed to be one of the masterminds of the Kennedy assassination. Beauboeuf had agreed to testify against Clay Shaw but later changed his mind.

where Beauboeuf was questioned by a "retired" intelligence officer in the offices of the Justice Department. This trip was paid for, as are the lawyer's legal fees, by the CIA—in other words, with our tax dollars.

Another lawyer, Stephen Plotkin, who represents Gordon Novel[3] [another of Garrison's key witnesses], has admitted he is paid by the CIA—and has also admitted his client is a CIA agent; you may have seen that story on page 96 of The New York Times, next to ship departures. Plotkin, incidentally, sued me for $10,000,000 for defaming his client and sued a group of New Orleans businessmen financing my investigation for $50,000,000—which meant, in effect, that the CIA was suing us. As if they need the money. But my attorney filed a motion for a deposition to be taken from Novel, which meant that he would have to return to my jurisdiction to file his suit and thus be liable for questioning in the conspiracy case. Rather than come down to New Orleans and face the music, Novel dropped his suit and sacrificed a possible $60,000,000 judgment. Now, there's a man of principle; he knows there are some things more important than money.

PLAYBOY: Do you also believe Clay Shaw's lawyers are being paid by the CIA?

GARRISON: I can't comment directly on that, since it relates to Shaw's trial. But I think the clincher, as far as Washington's obstruction of our probe goes, is the consistent refusal of the Federal Government to make accessible to us any information about the roles of the CIA, anti-Castro Cuban exiles and the para-military right in the assassination. There is, without doubt, a conspiracy by elements of the Federal Government to keep the facts of this case from ever becoming known—a conspiracy that is the logical extension of the initial conspiracy by the CIA to conceal vital evidence from the Warren Commission.

PLAYBOY: What "vital evidence" did the CIA withhold

3. Gordon Novel was a CIA employee, a friend of David Ferrie, and a consultant to Walter Sheridan; he was extradited from Ohio to testify during Shaw's trial.

from the Warren Commission?

GARRISON: A good example is Commission Exhibit number 237. This is a photograph of a stocky, balding, middle-aged man published without explanation or identification in the 26 volumes of the Warren Report. There's a significant story behind Exhibit number 237. Throughout the late summer and fall of 1963, Lee Oswald was shepherded in Dallas and New Orleans by a CIA "baby sitter" who watched over Oswald's activities and stayed with him. My office knows who he is and what he looks like.

Oswald Worked for the CIA

PLAYBOY: Are you implying that Oswald was working for the CIA?

GARRISON: Let me finish and you can decide for yourself. When Oswald went to Mexico City in an effort to obtain a visa for travel to Cuba, this CIA agent accompanied him. Now, at this particular time, Mexico was the only Latin-American nation maintaining diplomatic ties with Cuba, and leftists and Communists from all over the hemisphere traveled to the Cuban Embassy in Mexico City for visas to Cuba. The CIA, quite properly, had placed a hidden movie camera in a building across the street from the embassy and filmed everyone coming and going. The Warren Commission, knowing this, had an assistant legal counsel ask the FBI for a picture of Oswald and his companion on the steps of the embassy, and the FBI, in turn, filed an affidavit saying they had obtained the photo in question from the CIA. The only trouble is that the CIA supplied the Warren Commission with a phony photograph. The photograph of an "unidentified man" published in the 26 volumes is not the man who was filmed with Oswald on the steps of the Cuban Embassy, as alleged by the CIA. It's perfectly clear that the actual picture of Oswald and his companion was suppressed and a fake photo substituted because the second man in the picture was working for the CIA in 1963, and his identification as a CIA agent would have opened up a whole can of worms about Oswald's ties with the Agency. To prevent this, the CIA presented the Warren Commission with fraudulent evidence—a pattern that repeats itself whenever the CIA submits evidence relating to Oswald's possible connection with any U.S. intelligence agency. The CIA lied to the Commission right down the line; and since the Warren Commission had no investigative staff of its own but had to rely on the FBI, the Secret Service and the CIA for its evidence, it's understandable why the Commission concluded that Oswald had no ties with American intelligence agencies.

PLAYBOY: What was the nature of these ties?

GARRISON: That's not altogether clear, at least insofar as his specific assignments are concerned; but we do have proof that Oswald was recruited by the CIA in his Marine Corps days, when he was mysteriously schooled in Russian and allowed to subscribe to Pravda. And shortly before his trip to the Soviet Union, we have learned, Oswald was trained as an intelligence agent at the CIA installation at Japan's Atsugi Air Force Base—which may explain why no disciplinary action was taken against him when he returned to the U.S. from the Soviet Union, even though he had supposedly defected with top-secret information about our radar networks. The money he used to return to the U.S., incidentally, was advanced to him by the State Department. . . .

PLAYBOY: John A. McCone, former director of the Central Intelligence Agency, has said of Oswald: "The Agency never contacted him, interviewed him, talked with him or received or solicited any reports or information from him or communicated with him in any manner. Lee Harvey Oswald was never associated or connected directly or indirectly, in any way whatsoever, with the Agency." Why do you refuse to accept McCone's word?

GARRISON: The head of the CIA, it seems to me, would think long and hard before he admitted that former employees of his had been involved in the murder of the President of the United States—even if they weren't acting on behalf of the Agency when they did it. In any case, the CIA's past record hardly induces faith in the Agency's veracity. CIA officials lied about their role in the overthrow of the Arbenz Guzman regime in Guatemala; they lied about their role in the overthrow of Mossadegh in Iran; they lied about their role in the abortive military revolt against Sukarno in 1958; they lied about the U-2 incident; and they certainly lied about the Bay of Pigs. If the CIA is ready to lie even about its successes—as in Guatemala and Iran—do you seriously believe its director would tell the truth in a case as explosive as this? Of course, CIA officials grow so used to lying, so steeped in deceit, that after a while I think they really become incapable of distinguishing truth and falsehood. Or, in an Orwellian sense, perhaps they come to believe that truth is what contributes to national security, and falsehood is anything detrimental to national security. John McCone would swear he's a Croatian dwarf if he thought it would advance the interests of the CIA—which he automatically equates with the national interest.

Anti-Castro Cubans Killed Kennedy

PLAYBOY: Accepting for a moment your contention that there was a conspiracy to assassinate President John Kennedy, have you been able to discover who was involved—in addition to Ferrie[4]—how it was done and why?

GARRISON: Yes, I have. President Kennedy was killed for one reason: because he was working for a reconciliation with the U.S.S.R. and Castro's Cuba. His assassins were a group of fanatic anti-Communists with a fusion of interests in preventing Kennedy from achieving peaceful relations with the Communist world.

On the operative level of the conspiracy, you find anti-Castro Cuban exiles who never forgave Kennedy for failing to send in U.S. air cover at the Bay of Pigs and who feared that the thaw following the Missile Crisis in October 1962 augured the total frustration of their plans to liberate

---

4. David Ferrie was alleged by Garrison to have been one of the masterminds of the Kennedy assassination. By the time Garrison brought Shaw to trial, Ferrie had died under mysterious circumstances.

Cuba. They believed sincerely that Kennedy had sold them out to the Communists.

On a higher, control level, you find a number of people of ultra-right-wing persuasion—not simply conservatives, mind you, but people who could be described as neo-Nazi, including a small clique that had defected from the Minutemen because it considered the group "too liberal." These elements had their canteens ready and their guns loaded; they lacked only a target. After Kennedy's domestic moves toward racial integration and his attempts to forge a peaceful foreign policy, as exemplified by his signing of the Nuclear Test Ban Treaty, they found that target.

So both of these groups had a vital stake in changing U.S. foreign policy—ideological on the part of the paramilitary rightists and both ideological and personal with the anti-Castro exiles, many of whom felt they would never see their homes again if Kennedy's policy of détente was allowed to succeed. The CIA was involved with both of these

Jim Garrison (right) questioned the findings of the Warren Commission and investigated the theory of a conspiracy to kill the president.

groups. In the New Orleans area, where the conspiracy was hatched, the CIA was training a mixed bag of Minutemen, Cuban exiles and other anti-Castro adventurers north of Lake Pontchartrain for a foray into Cuba and an assassination attempt on Fidel Castro. David Ferrie, who operated on the "command" level of the ultra-rightists, was deeply involved in this effort.

The CIA itself apparently did not take the détente too seriously until the late summer of 1963, because it maintained its financing and training of anti-Castro adventurers. There was, in fact, a triangulation of CIA-supported anti-Castro activity between Dallas—where Jack Ruby was involved in collecting guns and ammunition for the underground—and Miami and New Orleans, where most of the training was going on. But then, Kennedy, who had signed a secret agreement with Khrushchev after the Missile Crisis pledging not to invade Cuba if Russia would soft-pedal Castro's subversive activities in the Americas, began to crackdown on CIA operations against Cuba. As a result, on July 31, 1963, the FBI raided the headquarters of the group of Cuban exiles and Minutemen training north of Lake Pontchartrain and confiscated all their guns and ammunition—despite the fact that the operation had the sanction of the CIA. This action may have sealed Kennedy's fate.

By the early fall of 1963, Kennedy's plan for a détente with Cuba was in high gear. Ambassador William Attwood, a close personal friend of the late President, recounts that a thaw in U.S.-Cuban relations was definitely in the works at this time and "the President more than the State Department was interested in exploring the [Cuban] overture." One of the intermediaries between Castro and Kennedy was the late television commentator Lisa Howard, who met secretly with Ernesto Che Guevara to prepare peace terms between the U.S. and Castro. Miss Howard was arranging a conference between Bobby Kennedy and Guevara when the President was shot in Dallas. In a United Nations speech on October 7, 1963, Adlai Stevenson set forth the possibility of a termination of hostilities between the two countries, and on November 19th, Presidential aide McGeorge Bundy, who was acting as an intermediary in the secret discussions, told Ambassador Attwood that the President wanted to discuss his plans for a Cuban-American détente in depth with him right after "a brief trip to Dallas." The rest is history. One of the two heads of state involved in negotiating that détente is now dead, but the survivor, Fidel Castro, said on November 23rd that the assassination was the work of "elements in the U.S. opposed to peace," and the Cuban Foreign Ministry officially charged that "the Kennedy assassination was a provocation against world peace perfectly and minutely prepared by the most reactionary sectors of the United States."

Most Americans at the time, myself included, thought this was just Communist propaganda. But Castro knew what he was talking about. A few weeks after the assassination, the Cuban ambassador to the UN, Dr. Carlos Lechuga, was instructed by Castro to begin "formal discussions" in the hope that Kennedy's peace plan would be carried on by his successor. Ambassador Attwood writes that "I informed Bundy and later was told that the Cuban exercise would be put on ice for a while—which it was and where it has been ever since." The assassins had achieved their aim.

PLAYBOY: This is interesting speculation, but isn't that all it is—speculation?

GARRISON: No, because we know enough about the key individuals involved in the conspiracy—Latins and Americans alike—to know that this was their motive for the murder of John Kennedy.

First of all, you have to understand the mentality of these people. Take the Cuban exiles involved; here are men, some of whom survived the Bay of Pigs, who for years had been whipped up by the CIA into a frenzy of anti-Castro hatred and who had been solemnly assured by American intelligence agencies that they were going to liberate their homeland with American support. They had one disappointment after another—the Bay of Pigs debacle, the failure to invade Cuba during the Missile Crisis, the effective crushing of their underground in Cuba by Castro's secret police. But they kept on hoping, and the CIA kept fanning their hopes.

Kennedy Died Because He Wanted Peace

Then they listened to Kennedy's famous speech at American University on June 10, 1963, where he really kicked off the new drive for a détente, and they heard the President of the country in which they'd placed all their hope saying we must make peace with the Communists, since "we both breathe the same air." Well, this worries them, but the CIA continues financing and training their underground cadres, so there is still hope. And then suddenly, in the late summer of 1963, the CIA is forced by Presidential pressure to withdraw all funds and assistance from the Cuban exiles. Think of the impact of this, particularly on the group here in New Orleans, which had been trained for months to make an assassination attempt on Castro and then found itself coolly jettisoned by its benefactors in Washington. These adventurers were worked up to a fever pitch; and when the CIA withdrew its support and they couldn't fight Castro, they picked their next victim—John F. Kennedy. That, in a nutshell, is the genesis of the assassination. President Kennedy died because he wanted peace.

A House Select Committee Believes a Conspiracy May Have Occurred

House Select Committee on Assassinations

Despite the findings of the Warren Commission that Oswald had acted alone, many Americans continued to believe that Oswald had had at least one accomplice. Nothing did more to fuel this belief than the testimony of twenty-one onlookers who claimed they had heard or seen something suspicious from the grassy knoll, a landscaped slope on the north side of Dealey Plaza. The Warren Commission had interviewed the onlookers but dismissed their testimony as confused and inconclusive. In 1976 the U.S. House of Representatives created a select committee on assassinations, known as the House Select Committee on Assassinations (HSCA), to investigate further the deaths of John Kennedy, Robert Kennedy, and Martin Luther King Jr.

As part of its work concerning the Kennedy assassination, the HSCA reconsidered the testimony of those witnesses who claimed that shots were fired from the grassy knoll. In addition, the HSCA obtained a tape made by the Dallas Police Department of the transmissions made over its channels during the assassination. The tape was submitted for acoustical analysis to a consulting firm to see if it had recorded any more shots than the three everyone agreed had been fired by Oswald. This article is an excerpt from the HSCA's final report concerning the assassination. In it the HSCA concludes that a fourth shot was indeed fired from the grassy knoll.

House Select Committee on Assassinations, "HSCA Final Assassinations Report," Assassination Archives and Record Center, www.aarclibrary.org, November 2001.

As you read, consider the following questions:
1. Do you agree with the HSCA's conclusion that, based on the Dallas Police Department dispatch tape, four shots were fired, one of them from the grassy knoll? If so, why? If not, why not?
2. How convincing is the testimony of the witnesses who believed they heard a shot fired from the grassy knoll? How well does this testimony support the HSCA's conclusion that a shot was fired from the grassy knoll?

The committee tried to take optimum advantage of scientific analysis in exploring issues concerning the assassination. In many cases, it was believed that scientific information would be the most reliable information available, since some witnesses had died and the passage of time had caused the memories of remaining witnesses to fail and caused other problems affecting the trustworthiness of their testimony.

As noted in the preceding section of this report, the committee turned to science as a major source of evidence for its conclusion that Lee Harvey Oswald fired three shots from the Texas School Book Depository, two of which hit President Kennedy. The evidence that was most relied upon was developed by committee panels specializing in the fields of forensic pathology, ballistics, neutron activation, analysis, handwriting identification, photography and acoustics. Of these, acoustics—a science that involves analysis of the nature and origin of sound impulses—indicated that the shots from the book depository were not the only ones fired at President Kennedy. . . .

Analysis by Bolt Beranek and Newman.—In order to identify the nature and origin of sound impulses in a recording, acoustical analysis may include, among other means of examination, a delineation and study of the shape of its electrical waveforms and a precise measurement and study of the timing of impulses on the recording. In May 1978, the committee contracted with Bolt Beranek and

Newman Inc. (BBN) of Cambridge, Mass. to perform this sort of analysis. The study was supervised by Dr. James E. Barger, the firm's chief scientist.

Bolt Beranek and Newman specializes in acoustical analysis and performs such work as locating submarines by analyzing underwater sound impuses. It pioneered the technique of using sound recordings to determine the timing and direction of gunfire in an analysis of a tape that was recorded during the shootings at Kent State University in 1970. In a criminal case brought against members of the National Guard by the Department of Justice, the analysis of the tape by BBN, combined with photographs taken at the time of the shootings, were used by the prosecution in its presentation to a grand jury to help establish which guardsmen were the first to fire shots. The firm was also selected by Judge John J. Sirica to serve on a panel of technical experts that examined the Watergate tapes in 1973.

The Dallas police dispatch materials given to BBN to analyze in May 1978 were as follows: The original Dictabelt recordings made on November 22, 1963, of transmissions over channel 1; A tape recording of channel 1 Dictabelts; A tape recording of transmissions over channel 2. . . .

BBN was asked to examine the channel 1 Dictabelts and the tape that was made of them to see if it could determine: (1) if they were, in fact, recorded transmissions from a motorcycle with a microphone stuck in the "on" position in Dealey Plaza; (2) if the sounds of shots had been, in fact, recorded; (3) the number of shots; (4) the time interval between the shots; (5) the location of the weapon or weapons used to fire the shots; and (6) the type of weapon or weapons used.

BBN converted the sounds on the tape into digitized waveforms and produced a visual representation of the waveforms. By employing sophisticated electronic filters, BBN filtered out "repetitive noise," such as repeated firings of the pistons of the motorcycle engine. It then examined the tape for "sequences of impulses" that might be significant. (A "sequence of impulses" might be caused by a loud noise—such as gunfire—followed by the echoes from that loud noise.) Six sequences of impulses that could have been caused by a noise such as gunfire were initially identified as having been transmitted over channel 1. Thus, they warranted further analysis. . . .

An Acoustical Reconstruction

BBN next recommended that the committee conduct an acoustical reconstruction of the assassination in Dealey Plaza to determine if any of the six impulse patterns on the dispatch tape were caused by shots and, if so, if the shots were fired from the Texas School Book Depository or the grassy knoll. The reconstruction would entail firing from two locations in Dealey Plaza—the depository and the knoll—at particular target locations and recording the sounds through numerous microphones. The purpose was to determine if the sequences of impulses recorded during the reconstruction would match any of those on the dispatch tape. If so, it would be possible to determine if the impulse patterns on the dispatch tape were caused by shots fired during the assassination from shooter locations in the depository and on the knoll. . . .

The committee authorized an acoustical reconstruction, to be conducted on August 20, 1978. Four target locations were selected, based on: The estimated positions of the Presidential limousine according to a correlation of the channel 1 transmissions with the Zapruder film,[1] indicating that the first shot was fired between Zapruder frames 160 and 170 and that the second shot was fired between Zapruder frames 190 and 200; the position of the President at the time of the fatal head shot (Zapruder frame 312); and evidence that a curb in Dealey Plaza may have been struck by a bullet during the assassination. Two shooter locations were selected for the reconstruction: The sixth floor south-

1. Abraham Zapruder made a home movie of the presidential motorcade as it passed through Dealey Plaza. Known as the Zapruder film, it consists of 486 frames and is twenty-six and a half seconds long, and it captured the President's death on film.

east corner window of the Texas School Book Depository, since substantial physical evidence and witness testimony indicated shots were fired from this location; and the area behind a picket fence atop the grassy knoll, since there was considerable witness testimony suggesting shots were fired from there.

A Mannlicher-Carcano rifle was fired from the depository, since it was the type of weapon found on the sixth floor on November 22, 1963. Both a Mannlicher-Carcano (chosen mainly because it fires a medium velocity supersonic bullet) and a pistol, which fires a subsonic bullet, were fired from the grassy knoll, since there was no evidence in August 1978 as to what type of weapon, if any, may have been fired from there on November 22, 1963. Microphones to record the test shots were placed every 18 feet in 36 different locations along the motorcade route where a motorcycle could have been transmitting during the assassination.

A recording was made of the sounds received at each microphone location during each test shot, making a total of 432 recordings of impulse sequences (36 microphone locations times 12 shots), or "acoustical fingerprints," for various target-shooter-microphone combinations. Each recorded acoustical fingerprint was then compared with each of the six impulse patterns on the channel 1 dispatch tape to see if and how well the significant points in each impulse pattern matched up. The process required a total of 2,592 comparisons (432 recordings of impulse sequences times six impulse patterns). . . .

Of the 2,592 comparisons between the six sequences of impulses on the 1963 police dispatch tape and the sequences obtained during the acoustical reconstruction in August 1978, 15 had a sufficient number of matching points (a correlation coefficient of .6 or higher) to be considered significant. The first and sixth sequence of impulses on the dispatch tape had no matches with a correlation coefficient over .5. The second sequence of impulses on the dispatch tape had four significant matches, the third sequence had five, the fourth sequence had three, and the fifth sequence had three. Accordingly, impulses one and six on the dispatch tape did not pass the most rigorous acoustical test and were deemed not to have been caused by gunfire from the Texas School Book Depository or grassy knoll. Additional analysis of the remaining four impulse sequences was still necessary before any of them could be considered as probably representing gunfire from the Texas School Book Depository or the grassy knoll. . . .

Weiss-Aschkenasy analysis.—In mid-September 1978, the committee asked Weiss and Aschkenasy,[2] the acoustical analysts who had reviewed Barger's work, if they could go beyond what Barger had done to determine with greater certainty if there had been a shot from the grassy knoll. Weiss and Aschkenasy conceived an analytical extension of Barger's work that might enable them to refine the probability estimate. They studied Dealey Plaza to determine which structures were most [likely] to have caused the echoes received by the microphone in the 1978 acoustical reconstruction that had recorded the match to the shot from the grassy knoll. They verified and refined their identifications of echo-generating structures by examining the results of the reconstruction. And like BBN, since they were analyzing the arrival time of echoes, they made allowances for the temperature differential, because air temperature affects the speed of sound. Barger then reviewed and verified the identification of echo-generating sources by Weiss and Aschkenasy.

Once they had identified the echo-generating sources for a shot from the vicinity of the grassy knoll and a microphone located near the point indicated by Barger's tests, it was possible for Weiss and Aschkenasy to predict precisely what impulse sequences (sound fingerprints) would have been created by various specific shooter and microphone

2. Mark Weiss and Ernest Aschkenasy were acoustical experts. Weiss had examined White House tape recordings in conjunction with the Watergate grand jury investigation, while Aschkenasy had developed computer programs for analyzing large volumes of acoustical data.

locations in 1963. (The major structures in Dealey Plaza in 1978 were located as they had been in 1963.) . . .

Approximately 10 feet from the point on the grassy knoll that was picked as the shooter location in the 1978 reconstruction and four feet from a microphone location which, Barger found, recorded a shot that matched the dispatch tape within ±6/1,000 of a second, Weiss and Aschkenasy found a combination of shooter and microphone locations they needed to solve the problem. It represented the initial position of a microphone that would have received a series of impulses matching those on the dispatch tape to within ±1/1,000 of a second. The microphone would have been mounted on a vehicle that was moving along the motorcade route at 11 miles per hour.

Weiss and Aschkenasy also considered the distortion that a windshield might cause to the sound impulses received by a motorcycle microphone. They reasoned that the noise from the initial muzzle blast of a shot would be somewhat muted on the tape if it traveled through the windshield to the microphone. Test firings conducted under the auspices of the New York City Police Department confirmed this hypothesis. Further, an examination of the dispatch tape reflected similar distortions on shots one, two, and three, when the indicated positions of the motorcycle would have placed the windshield between the shooter and the microphone. On shot four, Weiss and Aschkenasy found no such distortion. The analysts' ability to predict the effect of the windshield on the impulses found on the dispatch tape, and having their predictions confirmed by the tape, indicated further that the microphone was mounted on a motorcycle in Dealey Plaza and that it had transmitted the sounds of the shots fired during the assassination.

A Shot Was Fired from the Grassy Knoll
Since Weiss and Aschkenasy were able to obtain a match to within ±1/1,000 of a second, the probability that such a match could occur by random chance was slight. Specifically, they mathematically computed that, with a certainty

factor of 95 percent or better, there was a shot fired at the Presidential limousine from the grassy knoll.

Barger independently reviewed the analysis performed by Weiss and Aschkenasy and concluded that their analytical procedures were correct. Barger and the staff at BBN also confirmed that there was a 95 percent chance that at the time of the assassination a noise as loud as a rifle shot was produced at the grassy knoll. When questioned about what could cause such a noise if it were not a shot, Barger noted it had to be something capable of causing a very loud noise—greater than a single firecracker. Further, given the echo patterns obtained, the noise had to have originated at the very spot behind the picket fence on the grassy knoll that had been identified, indicating that it could not have been a backfire from a motorcycle in the motorcade. . . .

Witness Testimony on the Shots

The committee, in conjunction with its scientific projects, had a consultant retained by Bolt Beranek and Newman analyze the testimony of witnesses in Dealey Plaza on November 22, 1963, to advise the committee what weight, if any, it should give such testimony, and to relate the testimony to the acoustics evidence the committee had obtained.

The statements of 178 persons who were in Dealey Plaza, all of whom were available to the Warren Commission, were analyzed: 49 (27.5 percent) believed the shots had come from the Texas School Book Depository; 21 (11.8 percent) believed the shots had come from the grassy knoll; 30 (16.9 percent) believed the shots had originated elsewhere; and 78 (43.8 percent) were unable to tell which direction the shots were fired from. Only four individuals believed shots had originated from more than one location. . . .

The Warren Commission had available to it the same testimony concerning shots from the knoll, but it believed it should not be credited because of "the difficulty of accurate perception." The Commission stated, ". . . the physical and other evidence" only compelled the conclusion that at least two shots were fired. The Commission noted, however, that the three cartridge cases that were found, when taken together with the witness testimony, amounted to a preponderance of evidence that three shots were fired. Nevertheless, the Commission held, ". . . there is no credible evidence to indicate shots were fired from other than the Texas School Book Depository." It therefore discounted the testimony of shots from the grassy knoll.

While recognizing that the Commission was correct in acknowledging the difficulty of accurate witness perception, the committee obtained independent acoustical evidence to support it. Consequently, it was in a position where it had to regard the witness testimony in a different light.

The committee assembled for the purpose of illustration the substance of the testimony of some of the witnesses who believed the shots may have come from somewhere in addition to the depository. A Dallas police officer, Bobby W. Hargis, was riding a motorcycle to the left and slightly to the rear of the limousine. Hargis described the direction of the shots in a deposition given to the Warren Commission on April 8, 1964: "Well, at the time it sounded like the shots were right next to me. There wasn't any way in the world I could tell where they were coming from, but at the time there was something in my head that said that they probably could have been coming from the railroad overpass, because I thought since I had got splattered . . . I had a feeling that it might have been from the Texas School Book Depository, and these two places was (sic) the primary place that could have been shot from.". . .

Abraham Zapruder, since deceased, was standing on a concrete abutment on the grassy knoll, just beyond the Stemmons Freeway sign, aiming his 8 millimeter camera at the motorcade. He testified in deposition given to the Commission on July 22, 1964, that he thought a shot may have come from behind him, but then acknowledged in response to questions from Commission counsel that it could have come from anywhere. He did, however, differentiate among the effects the shots had on him. One shot, he noted, caused reverberations all around him and was much more pronounced than the others. Such a difference, the committee noted, would be consistent with the differing effects Zapruder might notice from a shot from the knoll, as opposed to the Texas School Book Depository.

A Secret Service agent, Paul E. Landis, Jr., wrote a statement on the shooting, dated November 30, 1963. Landis was in the follow-up car, behind the Presidential limousine, on the outside running board on the right. He indicated that the first shot "sounded like the report of a high-powered rifle from behind me, over my right shoulder." According to his statement, the shot he identified as number two might have come from a different direction. He said: "I still was not certain from which direction the second shot came, but my reaction at this time was that the shot came from somewhere, towards the front, right-hand side of the road." Another witness, S.M. Holland, since deceased, also noted signs of a shot coming from a group of trees on the knoll. Holland was standing on top of the railroad overpass above Elm Street. Testifying in a deposition to the Warren Commission on April 8, 1964, he indicated he heard four shots. After the first, he said, he saw Governor Connally turn around. Then there was another report. The first two sounded as if they came from "the upper part of the street." The third was not as loud as the others. Holland said: "There was a shot, a report. I don't know whether it was a shot. I can't say that. And a puff of smoke came out about 6 or 8 feet above the ground right out from under those trees. And at just about this location from where I was standing, you could see that puff of smoke, like someone had thrown a firecracker or something out, and that is just about the way it sounded. It wasn't as loud as the previous reports or shots." When counsel for the Warren Commission asked Holland if he had any doubts about the four shots, he said: "I have no doubt about it. I have no doubt about seeing that puff of smoke come out from those trees either."

These witnesses are illustrative of those present in Dealey Plaza on November 22, 1963, who believed a shot came from the grassy knoll.

Analysis of the reliability of witness testimony.—The committee also conducted, as part of the acoustical reenactment in Dealey Plaza in August 1978, a test of the capacity of witnesses to locate the direction of shots, hoping the experiment might give the committee an independent basis with which to evaluate what weight, if any, to assign to witness testimony. Two expert witnesses were asked to locate the direction of shots during the test, and Dr. David Green, the BBN consultant, supervised the test and prepared a report on the reactions of the expert witnesses.

Green concluded in the report, ". . . it is difficult to draw any firm conclusions relative to the reports of witnesses in the plaza as to the possible locus of any assassin." Nevertheless, he stated that "it is hard to believe a rifle was fired from the knoll" during the assassination, since such a shot would be easy to "localize." Green cited as support for his conclusion the fact that only four of the 178 Dealey Plaza witnesses pointed to more than one location as the origin of the shots.

In its evaluation of Green's conclusions, the committee considered the different circumstances affecting the expert witnesses in the test and the actual witnesses to the assassination. The expert witnesses in August 1978 were expecting the shooting and knew in advance that guns would be fired only from the Texas School Book Depository and the grassy knoll and they had been told their assignment was to determine the direction of the shots. Further, there was no test in which shots were fired within seven-tenths of a second of each other, so no reliable conclusion could be reached with respect to the possibility that such a brief interval would cause confusion. Dr. Green's report also reflects that even though the two trained observers correctly identified the origin of 90 percent of the shots, their own notes indicated something short of certainty. Their comments were phrased with equivocation: "Knoll? Over my head. Not really on knoll or even behind me"; "Knoll/underpass"; and "Knoll? Not really confident." Their comments, in short, frequently reflected ambiguity as to the origin of the shots, indicating that the gunfire from the grassy knoll often did not sound very different from shots fired from the book depository.

An analysis by the committee of the statements of witnesses in Dealey Plaza on November 22, 1963, moreover, showed that about 44 percent were not able to form an opinion about the origin of the shots, attesting to the ambiguity showed in the August 1978 experiment. Seventy percent of the witnesses in 1963 who had an opinion as to origin said it was either the book depository or the grassy knoll. Those witnesses who thought the shots originated from the grassy knoll represented 30 percent of those who chose between the knoll and the book depository and 21 percent of those who made a decision as to origin. Since most of the shots fired on November 22, 1963 (three out of four, the committee determined) came from the book depository, the fact that so many witnesses thought they heard shots from the knoll lent additional weight to a conclusion that a shot came from there.

The committee, therefore, concluded that the testimony of witnesses in Dealey Plaza on November 22, 1963 supported the finding of the acoustical analysis that there was a high probability that a shot was fired at the President from the grassy knoll.

A Senate Select Committee Detects a Cover-Up

Senate Select Committee to Study Governmental Operations with Respect to Intelligence Activities

In the wake of the Watergate scandal, the U.S. Senate appointed a select committee to investigate the activities of the nation's intelligence agencies. Known as the Church Committee after the name of its chairman, Senator Frank Church, the committee interviewed hundreds of witnesses and reviewed huge volumes of documents from the FBI, the CIA, the National Security Agency, and the Internal Revenue Service, among others. The committee released its findings in the form of fourteen volumes between 1975 and 1976; its work was eventually taken over by a standing Senate committee. One of the committee's many tasks was to investigate how the FBI, CIA, and other agencies handled the investigation of Kennedy's assassination.

In this article, an excerpt from the committee's final report, the committee concludes that Kennedy probably was not killed by a conspiracy. However, the committee further concludes that the national intelligence agencies did a poor job of investigating the possibility that he was, particularly in light of the CIA's attempts to assassinate foreign leaders, including Cuba's Fidel Castro.

As you read, consider the following questions:
1. Should the FBI and CIA have investigated the possibility that Kennedy's assassination was supported by the Cuban government in retaliation for the CIA's attempts

Senate Select Committee to Study Governmental Operations with Respect to Intelligence Activities, "Book V: The Investigation of the Assassination of President J.F.K.: Performance of the Intelligence Agencies," Assassination Archives and Record Center, www.aarclibrary.org, November 2001.

to assassinate Castro? If so, why? If not, why not?
2. In your opinion, why were the FBI and CIA not more open in their dealings with the Warren Commission?
3. In your opinion, does this document support or undermine the theory that a foreign government was behind Kennedy's death? Why or why not?

The Select Committee's investigation of alleged assassination attempts against foreign leaders raised questions of possible connections between these plots and the assassination of President John Fitzgerald Kennedy. Questions were later raised about whether the agencies adequately investigated these possible connections and whether information about these plots was provided the President's Commission on the Assassination of President Kennedy (the Warren Commission). As a result, pursuant to its general mandate to review the performance of the intelligence agencies, the Select Committee reviewed their specific performance with respect to their investigation of the assassination of the President.

The Scope of the Committee's Investigation

The Committee did not attempt to duplicate the work of the Warren Commission. It did not review the findings and conclusions of the Warren Commission. It did not re-examine the physical evidence which the Warren Commission had. It did not review one of the principal questions facing the Commission: whether Lee Harvey Oswald was in fact the assassin of President Kennedy.

Instead, building upon the Select Committee's earlier work, and utilizing its access to the agencies and its expertise in their functions, the Committee examined the performance of the intelligence agencies in conducting their investigation of the assassination and their relationships to the Warren Commission.

In the course of this investigation, more than 50 witnesses were either interviewed or deposed. Literally tens of thousands of pages of documentary evidence were reviewed at the agencies and more than 5,000 pages were acquired. In addition, the Committee relied a great deal on testimony taken during the course of its investigation of alleged plots to assassinate foreign leaders, especially testimony relating to knowledge of those plots.

The Committee has been impressed with the ability and dedication of most of those in the intelligence community. Most officials of the FBI, the CIA, and other agencies performed their assigned tasks thoroughly, competently, and professionally. Supervisors at agency headquarters similarly met their responsibilities and are deserving of the highest praise. Yet, as this Report documents, these individuals did not have access to all of the information held by the most senior officials in their own agencies. Nor did they control, or even influence, many of the decisions made by those senior officials, decisions which shaped the investigation and the process by which information was provided to the Warren Commission. Thus, it cannot be too strongly emphasized that this Report examines the performance of the senior agency officials in light of the information available to them.

Many potential witnesses could not be called because of limitations of time and resources. For this reason the Committee has relied a great deal on the documentary record of events. The Committee's Report distinguishes information obtained from documents from information it obtained through sworn testimony through citations, since the documentary records may not accurately reflect the true events. On the other hand, the Committee has on many occasions noted that witnesses may have no recollection of the events described in documents which they either prepared or in which they were mentioned.

The following Report details the evidence developed to date. The Report is intended to be descriptive of the facts the Committee has developed. The Committee believes the investigation should continue, in certain areas, and for that reason does not reach any final conclusions. Instead, the Select Committee has recommended that the Senate Committee on Intelligence continue this investigation in those areas where the Select Committee's investigation could not be completed.

Summary of the Committee's Work

In the days following the assassination of President Kennedy, nothing was more important to this country than to determine the facts of his death; no one single event has shaken the country more. Yet the evidence the Committee has developed suggests that, for different reasons, both the CIA and the FBI failed in, or avoided carrying out, certain of their responsibilities in this matter.

The Committee emphasizes that this Report's discussion of investigative deficiencies and the failure of American intelligence agencies to inform the Warren Commission of certain information does not lead to the conclusion that there was a conspiracy to assassinate President Kennedy.

Instead, this Report details the evidence the Committee developed concerning the investigation those agencies conducted into the President's assassination, their relationship with each other and with the Warren Commission, and the effect their own operations may have had on the course of the investigation. It places particular emphasis on the effect their Cuban operations seemed to have on the investigation.

However, the Committee cautions that it has seen no evidence that Fidel Castro or others in the Cuban government plotted President Kennedy's assassination in retaliation for U.S. operations against Cuba. The Report details these operations to illustrate why they were relevant to the investigation. Thus, the CIA operation involving a high-level Cuban official, code-named AMLASH, is described in order to illustrate why that operation, and its possible ramifications, should have been examined as part of the assassination investigation. Similarly, although Cuban exile groups opposed to Castro may have been upset with Kennedy administration actions which restricted their activities, the Committee has no evidence that such groups plotted the assassination.

Almost from the day Castro took power in Cuba, the

United States became the center of attempts to depose him. Cuban exiles, anti-communists, business interests, underworld figures, and the United States Government all had their own reasons for seeking to overthrow the Castro government. These interests generally operated independently of the others; but on occasion, a few from each group would join forces in a combined effort.

In April 1961, a force of Cuban exiles and soldiers of fortune backed by the CIA attempted an invasion of Cuba at the Bay of Pigs. In November of that year, the United States Government decided that further such overt paramilitary operations were no longer feasible, and embarked on Operation MONGOOSE. This operation attempted to use Cuban exiles and dissidents inside Cuba to overthrow Castro.

When the United States faced a major confrontation with the Soviet Union during the October 1962 Cuban missile crisis, it terminated MONGOOSE; the CIA's covert operations against Cuba were reduced; and the FBI and other agencies of government began to restrict the paramilitary operations of exile groups. This rather sudden shift against paramilitary activity of Cuban exile groups generated hostility. Supporters of some of these groups were angered by the change in government policy. They viewed this as a weakening of the U.S. will to oppose Castro.

Throughout this period, the CIA had been plotting the assassination of Castro as another method of achieving a change in the Cuban government. Between 1960 and early 1963 the CIA attempted to use underworld figures for this assassination. By May 1962, the FBI knew of such plots, and in June 1963 learned of their termination.

Following a June 1963 decision by a "Special Group" of the National Security Council to increase covert operations against Cuba, the CIA renewed contact with a high-level Cuban government official, code-named AMLASH. At his first meeting with the CIA in over a year, AMLASH proposed Castro's overthrow through an "inside job," with U.S. support. AMLASH considered the assassination of Castro a necessary part of this "inside job." Shortly after this meeting with AMLASH, Castro issued a public warning reported prominently in the U.S. press about the United States' meeting with terrorists who wished to eliminate Cuban leaders. He threatened that Cuba would answer in kind.

Five days after Castro issued this threat, the Coordinating Committee for Cuban Affairs, an interagency planning committee subordinate to the National Security Council's Special Group, met to endorse or modify then existing contingency plans for possible retaliation by the Cuban Government. Representatives of the CIA, and of the State, Defense and Justice Departments were on this Committee. The CIA representatives on this Committee were from its Special Affairs Staff (SAS), the staff responsible for Cuban matters generally and the AMLASH operation. Those attending the meeting on September 12 agreed unanimously that there was a strong likelihood Castro would retaliate in some way against the rash of covert activity in Cuba.

At this September 12 meeting this Committee concluded Castro would not risk major confrontation with the United States. It therefore rejected the possibility that Cuba would retaliate by attacking American officials within the United States; it assigned no agency the responsibility for consideration of this contingency.

Within weeks of this meeting the CIA escalated the level of its covert operations, informing AMLASH the United States supported his coup. Despite warnings from certain CIA staffers that the operation was poorly conceived and insecure, the head of SAS, Desmond Fitzgerald, met AMLASH on October 29, 1963, told him he was the "personal representative" of Attorney General Robert Kennedy, and stated the United States would support a coup. On November 22, at a pre-arranged meeting, a CIA Case Officer told AMLASH he would be provided rifles with telescopic sights, and explosives with which to carry out his plan. He was also offered a poison pen device.

Following the President's death, searches of FBI and CIA files revealed that Lee Harvey Oswald was not unknown to the intelligence agencies. In late 1959, the FBI opened a "security file" on Oswald after his defection to the Soviet Union. After Oswald's return to this country in June 1962, he was interviewed twice by FBI agents; on each occasion he repeatedly lied. He also refused to be polygraphed about his negative answers to questions of ties with Soviet intelligence. Yet the FBI closed the Oswald security case immediately after the second interview. The case was reopened in March 1963, but Oswald was not interviewed by the FBI until August 10, 1963, when he requested an interview after his arrest in New Orleans for disturbing the peace. On the occasion of this third interview, he again repeatedly lied to FBI agents. A month later Oswald visited Mexico City, where he visited both the Cuban and Soviet diplomatic establishments, and contacted a vice consul at the latter who was in fact a KGB agent. Despite receiving this information on Oswald's Mexico City activity, the FBI failed to intensify its investigative efforts. It failed to interview him before the assassination despite receiving a note from him warning the FBI to leave his wife alone.

Serious Investigative Deficiencies

Immediately after the assassination, FBI Director J. Edgar Hoover ordered a complete review of the FBI's handling of the Oswald security case. Within six days he was given a report which detailed serious investigative deficiencies. As a result of these deficiencies seventeen FBI personnel, including one Assistant Director, were disciplined. The fact that the FBI felt there were investigative deficiencies and the disciplinary actions it took were never publicly disclosed by the Bureau or communicated to the Warren Commission.

The evidence suggests that during the Warren Commission investigation top FBI officials were continually concerned with protecting the Bureau's reputation and avoiding any criticism for not fulfilling investigative responsibilities. Within weeks after the assassination, the FBI, at the urging of senior Government officials, issued a report concluding that Oswald was the assassin and that he had acted alone.

The Bureau issued its report on the basis of a narrow investigation focused on Oswald, without conducting a broad investigation of the assassination which would have revealed any conspiracy, foreign or domestic.

Despite knowledge of Oswald's apparent interest in pro-Castro and anti-Castro activities and top level awareness of certain CIA assassination plots, the FBI, according to all agents and supervisory personnel who testified before the Committee, made no special investigative effort into questions of possible Cuban government or Cuban exile involvement in the assassination independent of the Oswald investigation. There is no indication that the FBI or the CIA directed the interviewing of Cuban sources or of sources within the Cuban exile community. The division of the FBI responsible for investigating criminal aspects of the assassination, and not the division responsible for investigating subversive activities (including those of Cuban groups), was primarily responsible for the investigation and served as liaison to the Warren Commission.

Director Hoover himself perceived the Warren Commission as an adversary. He repeatedly remarked that the Commission, particularly the Chief Justice, was "seeking to criticize" the FBI and merely attempting to "find gaps" in the FBI's investigation. On two separate occasions, the latter immediately upon release of the Commission's Report, Director Hoover asked for all derogatory material on Warren Commission members and staff contained in the FBI files.

Neither the CIA nor the FBI told the Warren Commission about the CIA attempts to assassinate Fidel Castro. Allen Dulles, former Director of Central Intelligence, was a member of the Warren Commission and presumably knew about CIA plots during his tenure with the Agency, although he probably was unaware of the AMLASH operation. FBI Director Hoover and senior FBI officials also knew about these earlier plots. In July 1964, two months before the Warren Commission issued its 26-volume report of its investigation and findings, FBI officials learned that a Cuban official (not known to the Bureau as "AMLASH") was plotting with the CIA to assassinate Castro. However, there is no evidence this knowledge affected the FBI investigation of the President's assassination in any way. The Attorney General and other government officials knew there had been previous assassination plots with the underworld. None of the testimony or documents received by the Warren Commission mentioned the CIA assassination plots. The subordinate officers at the FBI and the CIA who acted as liaisons with the Warren Commission did not know of the CIA assassination attempts.

The AMLASH plot was more relevant to the Warren Commission's work than the early CIA assassination plots with the underworld. Unlike those earlier plots, the AMLASH operation was in progress at the time of the assassination; unlike the earlier plots, the AMLASH operation could clearly be traced to the CIA; and unlike the earlier plots, the CIA had endorsed AMLASH's proposal for a coup, the first step to him being Castro's assassination, despite Castro's threat to retaliate for such plotting. No one directly involved in either agency's investigation was told of the AMLASH operation. No one investigated a connection between the AMLASH operation and President Kennedy's assassination. Although Oswald had been in contact with pro-Castro and anti-Castro groups for many months before the assassination, the CIA did not conduct a thorough investigation of questions of Cuban Government or Cuban exile involvement in the assassination.

The AMLASH Plot Was Relevant to Kennedy's Assassination

CIA officials knowledgeable of the AMLASH plot testified they did not relate it to the President's assassination; however, those at CIA and FBI responsible for their agency's investigation testified that, had they been aware of the plot, they would have considered it relevant to their investigation. The individual who directed the CIA investigation for the first month after the assassination testified that he felt knowledge of the AMLASH operation would have been a "vital factor" in shaping his investigation. His successor at the CIA also stated that knowledge of the AMLASH plot would have made a difference in his investigation. Individuals on the Warren Commission staff have expressed similar opinions as to all plots against Castro. There is also evidence that CIA investigators requested name traces which should have made them aware of the AMLASH operation, but for some reason, they did not learn of that operation.

Although the Warren Commission concluded its work in September 1964, the investigation of the assassination was not to end. Both FBI Director Hoover and CIA Deputy Director for Plans Richard Helms pledged to keep the matter as an open case.

In 1965, the FBI and the CIA received information about the AMLASH operation, which indicated the entire operation was insecure, and caused the CIA to terminate it. Despite the fact that the information then received might have raised doubts about the investigation of the President's assassination, neither agency re-examined the assassination.

The assassination of President Kennedy again came to the attention of the intelligence agencies in 1967. President Johnson took a personal interest in allegations that Castro had retaliated. Although the FBI received such allegations, no investigation was conducted.

On the very day President Johnson received the FBI reports of these allegations, he met with CIA Director Richard Helms. The next day, Helms ordered the CIA Inspector General to prepare a report on Agency sponsored assassination plots. Although this report raised the question of a possible connection between the CIA plots against Castro and the assassination of President Kennedy, it was not furnished to CIA investigators who were to review the Kennedy assassination investigation. Once again, although these CIA investigators requested information that should have led them to discover the AMLASH operation, they apparently did not receive that information.

Findings

The Committee emphasizes that it has not uncovered any evidence sufficient to justify a conclusion that there was a conspiracy to assassinate President Kennedy.

The Committee has, however, developed evidence which impeaches the process by which the intelligence agencies arrived at their own conclusions about the assassination, and by which they provided information to the Warren Commission. This evidence indicates that the investigation of the assassination was deficient and that facts which might have substantially affected the course of the investigation were not provided the Warren Commission or those individuals within the FBI and the CIA, as well as other agencies of Government, who were charged with investigating the assassination.

The Committee has found that the FBI, the agency with primary responsibility in the matter, was ordered by Director Hoover and pressured by higher government officials, to conclude its investigation quickly. The FBI conducted its investigation in an atmosphere of concern among senior Bureau officials that it would be criticized and its reputation tarnished. Rather than addressing its investigation to all significant circumstances, including all possibilities of conspiracy, the FBI investigation focused narrowly on Lee Harvey Oswald.

The Committee has found that even with this narrow focus, the FBI investigation, as well as the CIA inquiry, was deficient on the specific question of the significance of Oswald's contacts with pro-Castro and anti-Castro groups for the many months before the assassination. Those individuals directly responsible for the investigations were not fully conversant with the fluctuations in American policy toward those who opposed Castro, and they lacked a working knowledge of pro-Castro and anti-Castro activity. They did not know the full extent of U.S. operations against Cuba including the CIA efforts to assassinate Castro. The Committee further found that these investigative deficiencies are probably the reason that significant leads received by intelligence agencies were not pursued.

Senior Bureau officials should have realized the FBI efforts were focused too narrowly to allow for a full investigation. They should have realized the significance of Oswald's Cuban contacts could not be fully analyzed without the direct involvement of FBI personnel who had expertise in such matters. Yet these senior officials permitted the investigation to take this course and viewed the Warren Commission investigation in an adversarial light.

Senior CIA officials also should have realized that their agency was not utilizing its full capability to investigate Oswald's pro-Castro and anti-Castro connections. They should have realized that CIA operations against Cuba, particularly operations involving the assassination of Castro, needed to be considered in the investigation. Yet, they directed their subordinates to conduct an investigation without telling them of these vital facts. These officials, whom the Warren Commission relied upon for expertise, advised the Warren Commission that the CIA had no evidence of foreign conspiracy.

Why senior officials of the FBI and the CIA permitted the investigation to go forward, in light of these deficiencies, and why they permitted the Warren Commission to reach its conclusion without all relevant information is still unclear. Certainly, concern with public reputation, problems of coordination between agencies, possible bureaucratic failure and embarrassment, and the extreme compartmentation of knowledge of sensitive operations may have contributed to these shortcomings. But the possibility exists that senior officials in both agencies made conscious decisions not to disclose potentially important information.

Because the Select Committee to Study Governmental Operations With Respect to Intelligence Activities ended on May 31, 1976, a final resolution of these questions was impossible. Nevertheless, the Committee decided to make its findings public, because the people have a right to know how these special agencies of the Government fulfill their responsibilities.

The Committee recommends that its successor, the Senate Select Committee on Intelligence, the permanent Senate Committee overseeing intelligence operations, continue the investigation in an attempt to resolve these questions. To assist its successor, this Committee has forwarded all files pertaining to this investigation.

This phase of the Committee's work will undoubtedly stir controversy. Few events in recent memory have so aroused the emotions of this Nation and the world, as those in Dallas, in November 1963. Conspiracy theories and theorists abound, and the public remains unsatisfied. Regrettably, this Report will not put the matter to rest. Even after additional investigative work, no additional evidence may come to light on the ultimate question of why President Kennedy was assassinated.

The Assassination Records Review Board Raises Questions

Assassination Records Review Board

Surprisingly, the Warren Commission paid little attention to President Kennedy's autopsy report. It stands to reason that the autopsy report would provide incontrovertible evidence as to exactly where and how many times Kennedy was shot, and yet the commission never seems to have reviewed this information. Moreover, the autopsy report was not released to the American public, and exactly what happened during the autopsy and what its findings were remain shrouded in mystery to this day.

In 1991 Hollywood director Oliver Stone released *JFK*. Stone has been widely criticized for this "fictional" version of the Kennedy assassination, although in fact it is a faithful presentation of Jim Garrison's version of the Kennedy assassination. In the wake of the controversy caused by *JFK*, the U.S. Congress passed the President John F. Kennedy Assassinations Record Collections Act of 1992, popularly known as the JFK Act. The act created the Assassination Records Review Board (ARRB) as an independent agency and assigned it the task of locating and making public as many documents relating to Kennedy's assassination as it could find.

This article is an excerpt from the ARRB's final report. In it the board outlines the difficulties it had in clarifying the record on the medical evidence and raises the possibility that parts of the autopsy report have been altered or destroyed.

Assassination Records Review Board, "AARB Final Report," Assassination Archives and Record Center, www.aarclibrary.org, November 2001.

As you read, consider the following questions:
1. Based on this excerpt, why might the Warren Commission not have reviewed the autopsy report more thoroughly?
2. To what degree, if any, does this excerpt support the contention that President Kennedy was killed by a conspiracy?

Many students of the assassination believe that the medical evidence on the assassination of President Kennedy, in concert with the ballistics evidence and film recordings of the events in Dealey Plaza, is the most important documentation in the case, as indeed it would be in any homicide investigation. The Review Board believed that, in order to truly address the public's concerns relating to possible conspiracies and cover-ups relating to the assassination, it would need to gather some additional information on all three of these topics. The pages that follow detail the Review Board's efforts to develop additional information on these highly relevant and interesting topics.

The *President John F. Kennedy Assassination Records Collection Act of 1992* (JFK Act) did not task the Assassination Records Review Board with the mission of investigating the assassination or of attempting to resolve any of the substantive issues surrounding it. But the JFK Act did authorize the Review Board to pursue issues related to the documentary record, including the completeness of records and the destruction of records. In an informal discussion with the Review Board, Congressman Louis Stokes, former Chairman of the House Select Committee on Assassinations (HSCA), strongly encouraged the Review Board to do what it could to help resolve issues surrounding the documentary record of the autopsy. He advised the Board that the medical evidence is of particular importance and that he hoped that it would do all it could to complete the record. Despite being hampered by a 33-year-old paper trail, the Review Board vigorously pursued additional records related to the medical evidence and the autopsy, commencing in 1996.

Medical Issues

One of the many tragedies related to the assassination of President Kennedy has been the incompleteness of the autopsy record and the suspicion caused by the shroud of secrecy that has surrounded the records that do exist. Although the professionals who participated in the creation and the handling of the medical evidence may well have had the best of intentions in not publicly disclosing information—protecting the privacy and the sensibilities of the President's family—the legacy of such secrecy ultimately has caused distrust and suspicion. There have been serious and legitimate reasons for questioning not only the completeness of the autopsy records of President Kennedy, but the lack of a prompt and complete analysis of the records by the Warren Commission.

Among the several shortcomings regarding the disposition of the autopsy records, the following points illustrate the problem. First, there has been confusion and uncertainty as to whether the principal autopsy prosector, Dr. James J. Humes, destroyed the original draft of the autopsy report, or if he destroyed notes taken at the time of the autopsy. Second, the autopsy measurements were frequently imprecise and sometimes inexplicably absent. Third, the prosectors were not shown the original autopsy photographs by the Warren Commission, nor were they asked enough detailed questions about the autopsy or the photographs. Fourth, the persons handling the autopsy records did not create a complete and contemporaneous accounting of the number of photographs nor was a proper chain of custody established for all of the autopsy materials. Fifth, when Dr. Humes was shown some copies of autopsy photographs during his testimony before the HSCA, he made statements that were interpreted as suggesting that he had revised his original opinion significantly on the location of the entrance wound. These shortcomings should have been remedied shortly after the assassination while memories were fresh and records were more readily recoverable.

The first step taken by the Review Board in regard to the

medical evidence was to arrange for the earliest possible release of all relevant information in the Warren Commission and HSCA files. Prior to the passage of the JFK Act, the files from the HSCA contained numerous medical records that had never been released to the public. After the JFK Act came into effect, but before the Review Board was created, the National Archives and Records Administration (NARA) released many of these records. Once the Review Board staff was in place in fall of 1994, it attempted to identify all remaining records that appeared to be connected to the medical evidence and arranged for their prompt release. All of these records were sent to NARA by early 1995 without redactions and without postponements.

The Review Board queried several government entities about possible files related to the autopsy, including the Bethesda National Naval Medical Center, the Armed Forces Institute of Pathology, the Naval Photographic Center, the Senate Select Committee on Intelligence (for Church Committee Records), and the President John F. Kennedy Library. The Review Board also attempted to contact all former staff members of the House Select Committee on Assassinations. With the exception of the autopsy photographs and x-rays, which are exempt from public disclosure under the JFK Act, the Review Board arranged for the release of *all* governmental records related to the autopsy. There are no other restricted records related to the autopsy of which the Review Board is aware.

The Review Board's search for records thereupon extended to conducting informal interviews of numerous witnesses, taking depositions under oath of the principal persons who created autopsy records, and arranging for the digitizing of the autopsy photographs.

There were many notable successes resulting from the Board's work, a few of which may briefly be mentioned here. With the generous and public-spirited cooperation of the Eastman Kodak Company, NARA, the FBI, and a representative of the Kennedy family, the Review Board was able to provide secure transportation to ship the autopsy photographs to Rochester, New York, to be digitized on the most advanced digital scanner in the world. The digitized images will be capable of further enhancement as technology and science advance. The digitizing should also provide assistance for those who wish to pursue the question of whether the autopsy photographs were altered. The Review Board also was able to identify additional latent autopsy photographs on a roll of film that had (inaccurately) been described as "exposed to light and processed, but showing no recognizable image." Again with the generous cooperation of Kodak, the latent photographs were digitized and enhanced for further evaluation. These digitized records have already been transferred to the John F. Kennedy Assassination Records Collection (JFK Collection) at NARA. Access to these materials is controlled by a representative of the Kennedy family.

Documents Missing or Nonauthentic

On another front, through staff efforts, the Review Board was able to locate a new witness, Ms. Saundra Spencer, who worked at the Naval Photographic Center in 1963. She was interviewed by phone and then brought to Washington where her deposition was taken under oath in the presence of the autopsy photographs. Ms. Spencer testified that she developed post-mortem photographs of President Kennedy in November 1963, and that these photographs were different from those in the National Archives since 1966. In another deposition under oath, Dr. Humes, one of the three autopsy prosectors, acknowledged under questioning—in testimony that appears to differ from what he told the Warren Commission—that he had destroyed both his notes taken at the autopsy and the first draft of the autopsy report. Autopsy prosector Dr. "J" Thornton Boswell, in an effort to clarify the imprecision in the autopsy materials, marked on an anatomically correct plastic skull his best recollection of the nature of the wounds on the President's cranium. The autopsy photographer, Mr. John Stringer, in detailed testimony, explained the photographic procedures he followed at the autopsy and he raised some questions about whether the supplemental brain photographs that he took are those that are now in NARA. His former assistant, Mr. Floyd Riebe, who had earlier told several researchers that the autopsy photographs had been altered based upon his examination of photographs that have been circulating in the public domain, re-evaluated his earlier opinion when shown the actual photographs at NARA.

Perhaps the most challenging aspect of the Review Board's work on the medical evidence was the preparation and taking of the depositions of the principal persons with knowledge about the autopsy and autopsy records. Although conducting such work was not required by the JFK Act, the Review Board sought to obtain as much information as possible regarding the documentary record. Accordingly, it identified all of the still-living persons who were involved in the creation of autopsy records and brought virtually all of them to NARA. For the first time, in the presence of the original color transparencies and sometimes first-generation black-and-white prints, the witnesses were asked questions about the authenticity of the photographs, the completeness of the autopsy records, the apparent gaps in the records, and any additional information in their possession regarding the medical evidence. The witnesses came from as far away as Switzerland (Dr. Pierre Finck) and as close as Maryland (Dr. "J" Thornton Boswell). In conducting the depositions, the Review Board staff sought to approach the questioning in a professional manner and without prejudging the evidence or the witnesses.

Near the end of its tenure, the Review Board also took the joint deposition of five of the Dallas physicians who treated the President's wounds at Parkland Memorial Hospital on November 22, 1963.

Fading Memories and Unreliable Testimony

There were three closely related problems that seriously impeded the Review Board's efforts to complete the documentary record surrounding the autopsy: a cold paper trail, faded memories, and the unreliability of eyewitness testimony. An example of the cold paper trail comes from Admiral George Burkley, who was President Kennedy's military physician and the only medical doctor who was present both during emergency treatment at Parkland Memorial Hospital and at the autopsy at Bethesda Naval Hospital. In the late 1970s, at the time of the HSCA's investigation, Dr. Burkley, through his attorney, suggested to the HSCA that he might have some additional information about the autopsy. Because Dr. Burkley is now deceased, the Review Board sought additional information both from his former lawyer's firm, and from Dr. Burkley's family. The Burkley family said it did not possess any papers or documents related to the assassination, and declined to sign a waiver of attorney-client privilege that would have permitted the Review Board access to the files of Mr. Illig (also now deceased), Burkley's former attorney.

Memories fade over time. A very important figure in the chain-of-custody on the autopsy materials, and the living person who perhaps more than any other would have been able to resolve some of the lingering questions related to the disposition of the original autopsy materials, is Robert Bouck of the Secret Service. At the time he was interviewed he was quite elderly and little able to remember the important details. Similarly, the records show that Carl Belcher, formerly of the Department of Justice, played an important role in preparing the inventory of autopsy records. He was, however, unable to identify or illuminate the records that, on their face, appear to have been written by him.

Finally, a significant problem that is well known to trial lawyers, judges, and psychologists, is the unreliability of eyewitness testimony. Witnesses frequently, and inaccurately, believe that they have a vivid recollection of events. Psychologists and scholars have long-since demonstrated the serious unreliability of people's recollections of what they hear and see. One illustration of this was an interview statement made by one of the treating physicians at Parkland. He explained that he was in Trauma Room Number

1 with the President. He recounted how he observed the First Lady wearing a white dress. Of course, she was wearing a pink suit, a fact known to most Americans. The inaccuracy of his recollection probably says little about the quality of the doctor's memory, but it is revealing of how the memory works and how cautious one must be when attempting to evaluate eyewitness testimony.

The deposition transcripts and other medical evidence that were released by the Review Board should be evaluated cautiously by the public. Often the witnesses contradict not only each other, but sometimes themselves. For events that transpired almost 35 years ago, all persons are likely to have failures of memory. It would be more prudent to weigh all of the evidence, with due concern for human error, rather than take single statements as "proof" for one theory or another.

CHRONOLOGY

1960
John F. Kennedy is elected president.

1961
Kennedy takes office.

1963
Kennedy is assassinated; Lee Harvey Oswald is charged with murdering Kennedy; Jack Ruby murders Oswald; President Lyndon Johnson appoints the Warren Commission.

1964
The Warren Commission Report declares that Oswald and Ruby had both acted alone.

1967
Orleans Parish, Louisiana, district attorney Jim Garrison charges Clay Shaw with conspiring to assassinate Kennedy.

1969
Shaw is tried and found innocent.

1975
The Zapruder film is shown to the public for the first time; the Rockefeller Commission investigates possible involvement by the CIA in Kennedy's death.

1976
The Church Committee concludes that the CIA and the FBI did not tell the Warren Commission everything they knew about Kennedy's death; House Select Committee on Assassinations concludes that Kennedy was killed by a conspiracy led by organized crime.

1991
Hollywood director Oliver Stone releases *JFK*.

1992
The JFK Act is passed, creating the Assassination Records Review Board (ARRB.)

1993
The National Archives and Records Administration releases more than twenty-one thousand pages of FBI files pertaining to the Kennedy assassination.

1998
ARRB issues its final report, which was preceded by the release of reams of declassified documents.

FOR FURTHER RESEARCH

Books

Bill Adler, *The Weight of the Evidence: "The Warren Report" and Its Critics.* New York: Meredith, 1968.

David W. Belin, *Final Disclosure.* New York: Charles Scribner's Sons, 1988.

Michael Benson, *Encyclopedia of the JFK Assassination.* New York: Facts On File, 2002.

G. Robert Blakey and Richard N. Billings, *The Plot to Kill the President: Organized Crime Assassinated JFK—the Definitive Story.* New York: New York Times Books, 1981.

Milton E. Brener, *The Garrison Case: A Study in the Abuse of Power.* New York: Clarkson N. Potter, 1969.

Howard L. Brennan and J. Edward Cherryholmes, *Eyewitness to History.* Waco, TX: Texan Press, 1987.

Walt Brown, *Treachery in Dallas.* New York: Carroll and Graf, 1995.

Thomas G. Buchanan, *Who Killed Kennedy?* London: Secker and Warburg, 1964.

Bob Callahan, *Who Shot JFK?* New York: Simon and Schuster, 1993.

Michael Canfield and Alan J. Weberman, *Coup d'État in America: The CIA and the Assassination of John F. Kennedy.* New York: Third Press, 1975.

John R. Craig and Philip A. Rogers, *The Man on the Grassy Knoll.* New York: Avon, 1992.

Albert B. Cunniff, *JFK Assassination: Nothing but the Truth.* Baltimore, MD: Books Unlimited, 1994.

John H. Davis, *The Kennedy Contract: The Mafia Plot to*

Assassinate the President. New York: HarperPaperbacks, 1993.

Jean Davison, *Oswald's Game.* New York: W.W. Norton, 1983.

Ovid Demaris and Gary Wills, *Jack Ruby.* New York: New American Library, 1968.

Judy Donnelly, *Who Shot the President?* New York: Random House, 1988.

James R. Duffy, *Who Killed JFK?* New York: Shapolski, 1988.

Michael H.B. Eddowes, *November 22: How They Killed Kennedy.* London: Neville Spearman, 1976.

Edward J. Epstein, *The Assassination Chronicles: Inquest, Counterplot, and Legend.* New York: Carroll and Graf, 1992.

George M. Evica, *And We Are All Mortal.* West Hartford, CT: University of Hartford Press, 1978.

James H. Fetzer, *Murder in Dealey Plaza: What We Know Now That We Didn't Know Then About the Death of JFK.* Peru, IL: Catfeet Press, 2000.

Gaeton Fonzi, *The Last Investigation.* New York: Thunder's Mouth Press, 1993.

Jim Garrison, *On the Trail of the Assassins.* New York: Sheridan Square Press, 1988.

Robert J. Groden and Harrison E. Livingstone, *High Treason.* New York: Berkley Books, 1990.

Henry Hurt, *Reasonable Doubt.* New York: Holt, Rinehart, 1986.

Connie Kritzberg, *Secrets from the Sixth Floor Window.* Tulsa, OK: Under Cover Press, 1994.

Michael L. Kurtz, *Crime of the Century: The Assassination from a Historian's Perspective.* Knoxville: University of Tennessee Press, 1982.

Mark Lane, *Rush to Judgement: A Critique of the Warren Commission's Inquiry into the Murders of President John F. Kennedy, Officer J.D. Tippit and Lee Harvey Oswald.* New York: Holt, Rinehart and Winston, 1966.

David S. Lifton, *Best Evidence: Disguise and Deception in the Assassination of John F. Kennedy.* New York: Penguin Books, 1992.

Harrison E. Livingstone, *Killing Kennedy and the Hoax of the Century.* New York: Carroll and Graf, 1995.

William Manchester, *The Death of a President.* New York: Harper and Row, 1967.

Priscilla J. McMillan, *Marina and Lee.* New York: Harper and Row, 1977.

Robert D. Morrow, *First Hand Knowledge: How I Participated in the CIA-Mafia Murder of President Kennedy.* New York: S.P.I. Books, 1992.

Oleg M. Nechiporenko, *Passport to Assassination: The Never-Before-Told Story of Lee Harvey Oswald by the KGB Colonel Who Knew Him.* New York: Birch Lane Press, 1993.

Gerald Posner, *Case Closed: Lee Harvey Oswald and the Assassination of JFK.* New York: Random House, 1993.

Bill Sloan and Jean Hill, *The Last Dissenting Witness.* Gretna, LA: Pelican, 1992.

Josiah Thompson, *Six Seconds in Dallas: A Micro-Study of the Kennedy Assassination.* New York: Bernard Geis, 1967.

Warren Commission, *The Warren Commission Report: The Official Report of the President's Commission on the Assassination of President John F. Kennedy.* Stamford, CT: Longmeadow Press, 1992.

Internet Sources

John McAdams, "The Kennedy Assassination." http:// mcadams.posc.mu.edu.

National Archives and Records Administration, "JFK Assassination Records." www.archives.gov.

Web Site

AARC: The Assassination Archives and Research Center, www.aarclibrary.org.

INDEX

assassination investigation by, 21, 22–23
Roosevelt, Franklin D., 33, 36, 66, 68
Royster, Vermont, 73
Ruby, Jack
  collected guns for the underground, 159
  jail behavior of, 96
  killer of Oswald, 14, 17, 30, 50–57, 133
  as lone gunman, 9, 28
  motive of, for killing Oswald, 16, 50, 56
  movements of, investigated, 134–35
  organized crime and, 26
  Senate investigation and, 147
Russell, Richard, 18

Salandria, Vincent, 142, 143
Sardar (horse), 62, 66
Sauvage, Leo, 122
Sawyer, Herbert J., 112
Sayre, Francis Bowes, Jr., 68
Schroder, Gerhard, 93
Secret Service, 32, 33, 36, 49, 52, 54
  experiment conducted by, 109
  protection for Johnson by, 68
Senate Select Committee to Study Governmental Operations with Respect to Intelligence Activities, 174
September 11, 2001, assassination likened to, 61
Shaw, Clay, 153
  arrest of, 149, 151
  assassination plot and, 22, 27, 28
  payment of lawyers by CIA, 154
Shepard, Tazewell T., Jr., 66
Sheridan, Walter, 150
Shires, Tom, 56
Shriver, Eunice Kennedy, 67
Shriver, Sargent, 67
Similas, Norman, 45, 48–49
Sirica, John J., 164
Skelton, Royce G., 112
Smith, Alan, 45, 49
Smith, Stephen E., 67
sound fingerprints, 167
sounds (gunfire), investigation of, 163–73
Soviets, ignored by conspiracists, 25

Soviet Union, 59, 178
  as adversary to U.S., 9
  aid of, to Cuba, 10
  Kennedy respected in, 77
  Oswald defected to, 20
Specter, Arlen, 144
Spencer, John S., 68
Spencer, Saundra, 191
Stevenson, Adlai, 83, 159
Stokes, Louis, 188
Stone, Oliver, controversial movie by, 22, 187
Stringer, John, 191
Sturgis, Frank, 23

Tague, James, 19, 30
Taylor, Maxwell D., 68
television
  Kennedy funeral watched by millions on, 15, 65
  Oswald shooting watched by millions on, 51
Texas School Book Depository
  acoustical reconstruction and, 165, 166, 167
  all shots fired from, 100–13, 123, 128
  beliefs about shots fired from, 169
  employees present when shots fired from, 106–109
  Oswald employee of, 14, 30
  rifle from sixth floor of, 13–14, 16, 32, 35, 101, 104, 105, 117–18, 127, 139
Time (magazine)
  on American mourning, 91–97
  on global mourning, 77–83
Tippit, J.D., killed by Oswald, 14, 16, 30, 118, 119, 128, 131, 132
Tippit, Mrs. J.D., 96–97
Trafficante, Santos, 24, 26
Triple Underpass, no shots fired from, 101, 109–13, 133
Truman, Harry S., 70
Tubman, William, 79
Turkey, nuclear warheads in, 9, 11

Underhill, J. Garrett, 152
Underwood, James, 103, 104, 105
United States
  Kennedy mourned by, 15
  tensions between Cuba and, 11
USSR. See Soviet Union